DOCTOR H.
AND
DOCTOR G.

HOW A HUSBAND-AND-WIFE TEAM OF PSYCHIATRISTS CAME
TO COLORADO AND HELPED TRANSFORM THE FIELD OF
MENTAL HEALTH

The life story of the innovative clinical psychiatrist, Dr. Gregorio
Kort, and Dr. Haydee Kort, the seventh superintendent and first
woman to head the Colorado State Hospital

AS TOLD TO JEAN TORKELSON

TESTIMONIALS FOR
DOCTOR H. AND DOCTOR G.

"In my life I've had the good fortune to have some outstanding mentors and administrators to look up to, and Haydee was one of them. Greg was a superb clinician who knew how to take care of very problematic patients. I don't think you could get that quality of care in Denver."

—- **Dr. Jay Scully, former vice chairman of the Department of Psychiatry at the University of Colorado and former Director of the Office of Education and Deputy Medical Director for the American Psychiatric Association.**

"Haydee was the best boss I ever had in my life and the best superintendent the hospital ever had."

—— **Dr. Elissa Ball, former Chief of Psychiatry at Colorado State Hospital**

"One of the main things to know about Greg and Haydee Kort is how incredibly supportive they were of the medical staff at the hospital. Their main objective was always to provide the best possible patient care, and they knew that to do that they had to support the physicians and staff who were providing that care. That came through very clearly over the years."

——- **Dr. Jay Richter, Chief of the Department of Medicine at the Colorado State Hospital from 1987 to 1994**

"The hospital really flourished under Haydee, and Greg was known for his skills at a psychiatrist ...together they are a wonderful couple."

—— Jacquie Huffaker, formerly at the Pueblo Chieftan newspaper and longtime friend of the Korts along with her husband, the late psychiatrist, Dr. Robert Huffaker

Dr. Gregorio Kort and Dr. Haydee Kort/Doctor H. and Doctor G.
Printed in the United States of America

Doctor H. and Doctor G./ Dr. Gregorio Kort and Dr. Haydee Kort -- 1st ed.

ISBN 978-0-578-42697-6 Print Edition

}

CONTENTS

"You came to the Colorado State Hospital
twenty-nine years ago,
touched the lives of patients, staff, and the families
and made CSH No. 1
as well as significantly enhancing
the entire Colorado Mental Health System

You will be greatly missed"

From the patients
and staff of CSH
June 6, 1990

The plaque presented to Dr. Gregorio Kort and Dr. Haydee Kort at their
retirement party, June 6, 1990

PREFACE

When Haydee and I stepped from the Argentine ocean liner, the *Rio Tunuyan,* into New York in 1957, all we had was our visas, two hundred dollars, and a pair of medical degrees from University of Argentina.

We were newlyweds in our early twenties, deeply in love, and known in Argentina to family, friends (and each other) as Goyo and Beba. As immigrants in New York, we were anonymous strangers who were still uncomfortable speaking English. But we shared a desire for adventure and the sense that, together, we could make something of ourselves in America.

As for *where* in America, or *how* we would do it, well, figuring that out was the challenge. We were approved to enter the U.S. on a visa program because we had been awarded physician internships at Nashville Memorial Hospital in Nashville, Tennessee. We didn't even know where Tennessee was, or what "living in the South" meant. We thought Nashville was a few hours' bus ride from New York. As for what branch of medicine we would specialize in, well, in those early days psychiatry was only one of many options.

We had left behind in Argentina our beloved parents and extended family, who greatly hoped we would return someday to practice medicine in our native country. They were hardy and talented people, immigrants themselves (originally from Poland), who overcame many challenges to create a better life for their children. In many ways, our story is their story too.

Of course, we did not return to Argentina. Within three years of arriving in America, Haydee and I were at the center of one of the most important advances in medical and psychiatric history. The pioneering moment followed the discovery in the mid-1950s of a new category of medical treatment for the mentally ill, the discovery of psychotropic drugs. These drugs, used either separately or in conjunction with existing treatments (such as psychotherapy), were the chemical balance wheel that stabilized many patients, offering the first hope and unprecedented opportunity for them to rejoin society and live full lives with their families and communities.

Until then, the overcrowded conditions in hospitals for the mentally ill were brutal and getting worse. As recently as 1951, ten years before we arrived in Pueblo, the overcrowded conditions at the Colorado State Hospital were so terrible that a story in one of Denver's two largest newspapers carried the melodramatic headline, "State Hospital City of the Damned."

Few professionals knew how to break up the old system. But we were privileged within our first years of coming to America to meet two unusual psychiatrists who *did* know how.

Dr. Luis Garcia-Bunuel and Dr. Willis Bower pioneered the concept of hospital decentralization and community-based treatment, a humane alternative to "warehousing" patients in glutted hospital wards. These groundbreaking leaders looked past our youth and immigrant status and recognized in us the same innovative spirit they had. By the time we interviewed for positions at their hospitals (first in Iowa, and then in Colorado), we were committed to following careers in psychiatry, and greatly intrigued by the concept of decentralization and the vision of these two men.

To be chosen to help make groundbreaking history would have been life changing enough, but Haydee and I were privileged to not only participate in this revolution but to pick up the torch and become leaders and innovators ourselves.

In 1977, Haydee was recognized for her exceptional executive skills when she was chosen to be the seventh superintendent to lead the Colorado State Hospital system. She was not only the first woman *in* the job, she was the best person *for* the job. During those years, Haydee inherited, and solved, a catastrophic budget crisis, navigated the rough seas of politics, and even managed to pull "small-town" Pueblo out of the shadow of Denver. Through her networking connections with the University of Colorado School of Medicine, Haydee transformed our hospital into the state's premier teaching hospital for resident psychiatrists.

The legacy Haydee created echoes to this day. In the summer of 2018 she was escorting guests to the hospital for a tour when one of the security guards (who was probably in high school during our working years there) stopped her at the front door and asked for credentials. "*You* are Dr. Haydee Kort?" he exclaimed. "The former superintendent? Welcome!" While we each have been honored with plaques placed in the building, the guard's enthusiasm for meeting Haydee in person spoke to her memorable leadership.

As for me, I was already working where I wanted to be, as the hospital's Director of Adult Psychiatric Services. As a practicing psychiatrist and department head, my role was to bring this new innovative system to my skilled staff, so together we could take the exciting concept of decentralization directly to the patients. Whether in the hospital setting or in the wider community, I was determined to create an environment where patients were treated as responsible, functioning adults. The result was groundbreaking ideas that included an award-winning, in-hospital art gallery, and outdoor adventures like camping and skiing trips, all done to emphasize to each mentally ill person that they were valued as human beings. These innovations led to astonishing improvements in their lives. For me, the crowning achievement and the goal of my career was to do everything I could to improve the environment of patients.

So for thirteen fulfilling years until our retirement in 1990, Haydee and I were privileged, each in our own way, to be able to advance opportunities and understanding for the mentally ill. Working along with us and bringing it all to life was the outstanding and dedicated staff at Colorado State Hospital.

Meanwhile, Haydee and I stuck to a commitment we made early in our marriage that we wanted to have a full family life too. Our informal rallying cry has always been, "Home by Five!" and it has paid off. Haydee and I have been able to sweeten our challenging careers with a happy marriage and the joy of sharing it with our two great children, Marcelo and Gabriela, and our cherished grandchildren, Stephanie, Andrew, Natalia and Sofia. To this day we treasure our many relatives, family, and friends in Argentina too, as well as in America, and especially in the city we have made our lifelong home, Pueblo, Colorado.

Over the years many people have been fascinated by the way Haydee and I have been able to work side by side, each in our own complementary spheres, with complete equanimity and lack of competition. All I can say is, I enjoyed being able to describe Dr. Haydee Kort, Superintendent of Colorado State Hospital, as "my boss," while Haydee was glad to have Dr. Gregorio Kort to turn to for free hospital consultations!

Together, of course, we will always be Goyo and Beba. However, there is another name for each of us we cherish just as deeply. It sprang up among the staff and patients of the Colorado State Hospital over our three decades at the hospital, and the name stuck. It reflects our close relationship with the many staff and patients we came to know and the affection we all felt for each other in our work.

During those challenging and fulfilling years we came to be known as "Dr. H. and Dr. G."

This is our story.

Dr. Gregorio Kort
October 2018
Pueblo, Colorado

CHAPTER ONE

"THE PROPER THING TO DO"

Gregorio Kort and Haydee Kantorovich caught each other's eye for the first time in a Jewish neighborhood club their families attended in La Plata, Argentina. Now, it's not surprising that a boy of 17 and a girl of 15 would find much in common and fall in love; each of them had an adventurous spirit and a desire to do well in life, and they came from close-knit families with high educational hopes for their children. What is striking about their first encounter in 1948 is that the strands of their families' histories began to entwine some eight thousand miles away, in the war-stressed country of Poland, and years before Gregorio and Haydee were born.

Gregorio's parents, Abram and Rosa Kort, arrived in Argentina in 1926 after enduring an exhausting two-month journey on a cargo ship jammed with refugees. Cradled in their arms was firstborn son, 10-month-old Marcos. The trip was all the more harrowing with a baby, not to mention under the harsh conditions of traveling third class, which was all Abram and Rosa could afford. Yet treasured in the family lore are stories of the great kindness of fellow emigres who helped Rosa take care of the baby and whisked lively little Marcos away at just the right moments so his weary mother could rest.

That same year, Haydee's father, Josel Kantorovich, boarded a ship in Poland also bound for Argentina. He was just 16 years old, and he was all alone. He came to Argentina at such a young age that for most of his life he called himself Jose. His destiny was to marry a girl born in Argentina, Sofia Schnizler, who was Haydee's mother.

Is it possible that these two families, strangers to each other but destined to be united someday, paced the same decks on the same ship on the same trip from Poland to Argentina? Yes, it is possible, though a definitive answer vanished long ago, along with the ship's manifests! What is known is that, for each family, in their own way, Argentina was to be their haven from persecution and the harsh storms of history.

From childhood, Gregorio was familiar with the story of his Polish-Jewish grandparents, Naftole and Din Kort. Even in the 1920s they saw that Poland's future was growing dark. They urged their children to flee Europe while they still could, because the continent was slowly being crushed in the vise of two catastrophes, one behind them, one still ahead.

The first catastrophe was World War I. Though it ended in 1918, it left Poland and much of Europe in economic shambles and political peril. That led to even greater dangers that began to build in the 1920s and '30s with the growing military power of the German Third Reich. It was becoming clear that the Nazi regime was determined to overrun Europe and fulfill one of its first priorities—the annihilation of the Jewish people.

"The proper thing to do was to get out of Europe, and my grandparents agreed about that," Gregorio said. "But they knew that they themselves could not leave. 'We cannot undertake that, we are too old to begin life over again in another country,' they said. Yet they were very wise people, and they understood what their children were facing if they stayed. They said, 'You must do this for yourselves and for your child, for Marcos,' even though they knew they would probably never see their children, or their grandchild, again."

Their sense of urgency was well placed. For Gregorio's grandparents, and all those who stayed behind in Poland, their sorrows deepened into tragedy.

"When Germany invaded Poland in 1939," Gregorio continued, "my grandparents still had a young daughter at home—my mother's younger sister—and she already had connections with all the young people in that little town in Poland, the town of Lulinietz, which was about twenty miles from Warsaw. The family began to make a plan: If the Germans invaded Poland, the young people would escape to Russia. And that is what happened. The Germans invaded Poland, and the young sister of my mother, along with all the young people in Lulinietz, all fled to Russia.

"My grandparents remained in Poland. They simply could not leave their homeland! Of course, as soon as the Germans invaded Poland, the Nazis immediately started cleaning house. First, they moved all the Jewish people into the ghetto, and then they started taking them to the gas chambers. And that was the fate of my grandparents, to die in the Holocaust."

∼

When Abram and Rosa left their homeland of Poland in 1926, that profound family tragedy was still some years away. But the young couple sensed the gathering storm, and they were eager to open a new family history in Argentina. At the time, the country was bursting with economic expansion and vigor, and it actively welcomed talented and hardworking refugees fleeing the coming Nazi oppression in Europe.

Abram and Rosa had first considered emigrating to the United States, but the immigration quotas of the day made it impossible to enter the USA immediately. For a young couple eager to build their future right away, Argentina was a happy alternative.

From their son Gregorio's earliest childhood, his parents impressed on him the great opportunities that Argentina offered their young immigrant family. "It was like the promised land," Gregorio said. "The country opened its arms to immigration. It was a huge country that was very receptive to immigrants. There were jobs and land to farm…"

There was another good reason to pick Argentina. Two of Rosa's brothers, Roberto and Zeliko Turkenich, were already in Buenos Aires, and each was finding a role in the country's wealth-building economy anchored by the livestock and meatpacking industries. Roberto worked in a leather company, and Zeliko was employed by the Swift meatpacking company. The Swift company, founded in the USA, distributed meat products worldwide. In cattle-rich, livestock-producing Argentina, the Swift company had virtually turned the capital city into a company town.

∾

In the same year of 1926, Haydee's father, Josel Kantorovich, age 16, began his journey from Poland to Argentina.

Josel (known forever after as Jose), came from a well-to-do family of physicians who had prosperous practices in Baranovich, Poland. In peaceful times, the young man could have expected that an equally prosperous and comfortable life would be his as well. But Jose didn't wait to find out, because he sensed his peaceful homeland was about to crack apart.

"His father was a doctor, and he had two brothers that were doctors," Haydee said. "But he left everything and decided to come to Argentina because he knew something was happening in Europe, and he wanted no part of it. And sure enough, they all went *kaput*. He never saw his family again."

Like his future relatives-in-law, Jose had applied first to emigrate to the United States, but like them, he was thwarted by U.S. immigration quotas. So he turned his attention to Argentina, the new "land of opportunity."

Imagine a harbor teeming with ships and barges, and hundreds of people a day being hurried off gangplanks into a bustling, brand-new world! Most of them carried bundles and shabby suitcases, and they wore the weary and careworn look of refugees everywhere. Mixed in with the clang and bang of crates and boxes and cargo, a thousand languages seemed to rise over the din, many if not most of them eastern European in origin: Polish, Russian, Yugoslavian, Yiddish…and Italian, French and German, too.

That was the chaotic scene that Josel Kantorovich, a Polish-Jewish teenager, stepped into on the roughened wooden docks of the Buenos Aires harbor in 1926. His first task was to look for what was known as a "displacement home," a rather depressing name for a kind of boarding house that took in refugees, or displaced persons. Actually, he was looking for a specific displacement home which he had been told about by an acquaintance in Poland: *"When you get to Buenos Aires, find Rosa's boarding home."* The home was run by a woman named Rosa Wernicke. Her family originally came from Germany, but she was happy to help all "displaced persons," especially those from neighboring Poland.

Already determined to fit in, the young man (who had already resolved to call himself Jose) found his way to the "displacement home" and marched up the steps. Surely his mind was racing with the questions facing every new immigrant—where would he find work? What was the path for getting ahead? How quickly would he be proficient in Spanish? For that hardworking generation, new-comers understood that assimilation was the fastest way to make a mark in their new country.

Little did Jose know that far from being a depressing first step on that journey, this "displacement home" in Argentina would be the doorway to a joyful, life-changing discovery:

The boarding house was run by his future mother-in-law!

Yes, that is where Jose Kantorovich met and fell in love with his future wife, Sofia Schnizler. Her mother Rosa had been married twice, the second time to a man named Wernicke. Now a widow, Rosa ran a boarding house, and her daughter worked there to help her mother.

Not only in courtship but also in his professional life, Jose Kantorovich quickly discovered Argentina to be the land of op-portunity indeed. A relative in Buenos Aires was a dentist, and this man took Jose under his wing and taught him the trade of becoming a "dental mechanic." In other words, he learned to make dentures. He became so good at it that he developed a real follow-ing in the dental trade. Eventually he opened his own lab and was able to hire several employees, all while he was still in his twenties.

The young Jose was establishing himself quickly in the professional world, and two years or so after arriving in Argentina, Jose and Sofia were married. In 1929 their son Alberto was born, and Haydee was born four years later, in 1933. With their two children, Jose and Sofia's family was complete, and they settled in the lively and sophisticated university town of La Plata, about thirty miles from Buenos Aires.

People often ask Haydee about her striking and beautiful name. She never heard an official explanation, except that it is French, and the accent should be on the first "e." In full, she was given the name Haydee Celia Kantorovich. But she was well known by her nickname, "Beba," which was pronounced "Bebbah."

The young man who was about to catch her eye in school had an unusual nickname, too. Everybody called him Goyo.

~

Slowly, year by year, the stage was being set for the meeting of two families, and the unfolding love story of Beba and Goyo— Haydee Kantorovich and Gregorio Kort.

But before the two teenagers met in 1948, their families had undergone many changes and challenges.

Haydee's family was already well established in La Plata, and her father Jose had an excellent professional reputation in the dental community. Haydee's mother, Sofia, had hoped to join the professional ranks by becoming a dentist, but she had serious physical problems with her spine which kept her in constant pain.

"She had several surgeries and while she could walk, she had so many physical problems that she could not do anything like go to school," Haydee said.

Despite Sofia's physical pain, she opened several stores. Her first store sold gifts and classical dancing equipment. Later, Sofia opened a clothing store.

Mother and daughter were very close. Sitting at her mother's knee, Haydee also learned at an exceptionally early age how to write and understand numbers. But that also led to a significant challenge in Haydee's young life.

"When I had just turned five, I wanted to go to school very badly, but my parents wouldn't let me because I was too young," Haydee recalled. "I guess I pestered my mother so much, that she decided to take me to the school, so the director of the school could tell me herself that I was too young to go! I simply would not take my mother's word for it.

"So one day we went to the school for our appointment with the school director. Now I had noticed this before, that the director wore a white uniform with buttons that had letters on them. That was my opening."

I said, "Why can't I go to school? I know all the letters on your buttons!"

"The director seemed impressed with that and she said, 'If she is so determined, let her come, and we will let her observe what the others do.' Then she took me by the hands and said, 'Just come!' So that's what I did."

Haydee was forever grateful to her mother for opening the door so she could take on that great challenge—and when she was just five years old! And although the school director's name is lost to memory, Haydee will never forget how she put a determined

5-year-old child on the path to lifelong learning: "She was very important in my life."

"After some months of observation, I ended up entering the first grade at the age of five, two years younger than the other students," Haydee said, adding with a smile, "the only downside was that I was so little, the teachers would pick me up in their arms and carry me around the school like a baby!"

Haydee was not treated as a "baby" for long. In her teen years, she took up ballet and piano, two pursuits that many well-to-do families in Argentina planned for their daughters. But Haydee was a cut above other girls her age; she proved to be exceptionally talented in both ballet and piano. She became a skilled pianist and a classical ballerina, and took solo lessons with a renowned dance instructor.

Haydee concentrated on classical ballet, and danced in productions of *Swan Lake* and other ballets by Tchaikovsky and other Russian composers. The family cherishes many photos of a beautiful young Haydee in tutu and *en pointe,* who was making a name for herself as a youthful ballerina, perhaps destined for a promising career. Whether ballet or piano, "That was my forte," she said. "I was drawn to it. My parents found the best possible teacher for ballet and the best possible teacher for piano, and I took lessons in both of them all through high school."

~

Meanwhile, the Kort family arrived in La Plata too, but only after a series of moves and adventures. They were not part of a professional community like the Kantorovich family; instead, they built their name and reputation by rising steadily in business as store proprietors.

Like Jose and Sofia Kantorovich, Abram and Rosa Kort were determined to succeed.

"My father was a go-getter," Gregorio said. The Kort family came from generations of merchants and salesmen in Poland. Rosa's father (Gregorio's grandfather) had owned a general store in a suburb of Warsaw, and the merchant route seemed like a good path to prosperity in Argentina, too.

However, that path presented unexpected twists and turns for Abram and Rosa. To begin, Rosa's two brothers, Roberto and Zeliko Turkenich, tried to get work for Abram in Buenos Aires, but a job didn't materialize right away. That led Gregorio to joke, "My parents came first to Buenos Aires, but they ended up in a country town with farmers!"

Eventually, Gregorio's parents would double back to Buenos Aires, but first they settled in a small farming district called General Villegas, which is located in the extreme northeast corner of the province of Buenos Aires. Here a determined young man could make a good living across the vast landscape selling much-needed goods door to door. For farm families living miles away from stores and cities, the sight of the salesman's truck rumbling down the dusty, worn roadway, with his traveling store of pots and pans, farm tools, sewing paraphernalia, cloth, and every necessity under the sun—well, that was a sweet sight indeed.

With the help of Rosa's brothers, Abram bought a small truck and began to crisscross the farmland selling goods door to door. The farm people were open, friendly and honest, and Abram and his customers sealed their transactions with a handshake. Abram's reputation for fairness and honesty made him a welcome sight to the farmers, and his traveling sales business prospered. At home, Rosa nurtured the family homestead, which eventually grew to four children. Marcos, the eldest, was born in Poland, followed by three siblings born in Argentina: Moises, Natalia, and Gregorio, the youngest, who in later years would often be known as Greg. He was born in the district of General Villegas in 1931.

Each child was born exactly two years apart, Gregorio noted, adding with a smile, "My parents were very well organized."

Then, when Gregorio was about four years old, a calamity struck the farming town. A plague of locusts descended on everything, blotting out the sun and destroying crops and any food left in the open. For every person in their path, "It was a terrible loss," Gregorio said. "The locusts came in such a huge number that they darkened the sun. Terrible! They ate everything. When they left, the bark of the trees was stripped away, and all the trees were white, like dead men's bones. We had chickens at the time, and they started laying green eggs because they were eating so many locusts.

"My parents had to wait it out," Gregorio said. "Of course, they weren't getting paid right away, because the farmers' crops were wiped out."

As Gregorio's father, Abram, started to assess the damage, he realized something. He was an honest and compassionate man, which made only one decision possible, even though it went against his own self-interest.

"I am not going to try to collect money from the farmers," he said. "They have nothing!"

The locusts had destroyed the farmers' crop harvest and

income, and left Abram without any customers. As it turned out, the terrifying locust plague was a great blessing in disguise for the Kort family. Yes, the traveling sales business had vanished, but the void allowed new opportunities to rush in.

Rosa's brothers had been looking out for the young family, and now they had a message for Abram. Whether they delivered it in Yiddish or Spanish is not known. But the meaning was clear: "We need to get you to Buenos Aires!"

So the brothers found an apartment in Buenos Aires for Abram, Rosa, and their lively family of four children. In the 1930s, the apartment resembled the capital city itself, which teemed with newcomers and refugees from all over the world.

But apparently the Kort family was a little *too* lively.

"We were all country kids," Gregorio recalled, "and at six a.m. we were up and playing and screaming and hungry. Finally the apartment managers told us, 'You have to get out, and if you won't, we will *get* you out.'"

Although the apartment didn't last long, "We had a lot of fun, I think," Gregorio said. "That's when my two uncles got to work to see what kind of job they could find for my father."

The job they found was a good one. Abram Kort became manager of a furniture store in Berisso, about fifty miles from Buenos Aires. Even better, as part of his compensation the manager was provided a house, which meant the Kort kids could finally spread out without worrying about complaining apartment neighbors

Instead, there were other things to worry about in the late 1930s. The world was inching closer to war, and in Europe, the Nazis were openly on the march. Directly in their path was Poland, and all those who were dear to the Kort and Kantorovich families.

"One of the things I remember is that my parents had a radio on all the time in the furniture store," Gregorio recalled. "With trepidation, they were following how the German troops were advancing, including when they invaded Poland and our town…"

Meanwhile in Argentina (which played a politically neutral game for as long as possible) life was bountiful. Huge boats jockeyed for position along the Río de la Plata riverbank, the entryway to the Buenos Aires harbor. Many carried immigrants from all parts of the world, others were headed out into the Atlantic Ocean, loaded with Argentina's rich surplus of livestock and meatpacking products. Some ships were bound for the USA and the Allied nations, others for Nazi Germany and the Axis powers.

In the town of Berisso, a young Gregorio Kort could stand on the banks of the mighty La Plata river (a major waterway for ships) and watch boats from all over the world make their way to and from the docks of Buenos Aires. The harbor was so shallow that the hugest ships were forced to wait offshore while barges delivered passengers and cargo on land. The sight of so many boats and ships lined up to enter and leave Buenos Aires was a memory Gregorio never forgot. The energy and vitality of those huge vessels, some bound for the Atlantic and parts unknown, others lining up to bring newly arrived immigrants to the Argentinian shores, was a thrilling sight. To a young man, it was like being at the center of everything, and the world was calling him to adventures he could not yet imagine.

"I loved it," he said.

～

Berisso was known as the immigrant capital of the world. Poles, Germans, Italians, Jews and Arabs, Russians and Czechs...every nationality was represented. In that day, instead of creating tension, ethnic diversity led to cooperation. "Everyone got along," Gregorio said. On busy days in the furniture store, the din of so many languages colliding together was a happy challenge. "How would I ever learn them all?" Greg recalled thinking.

In fact, it was no trouble at all to learn. The Kort kids made friends with children from all over the world, and many happened to be Italian immigrants. "We almost learned to speak Italian because we spent so much time eating with the Italian kids!" Gregorio said, with a laugh.

Gregorio's mother was also busy in the store, and they brought in an Italian lady to cook meals. "And my mother became an incredible Italian cook," Gregorio recalled. "She learned to do raviolis, gnocchi, everything from scratch."

As a young teenager, Gregorio worked for his father in the furniture store. It wasn't all sales work, ringing up cash registers and schmoozing customers; there was hard physical work to be done, too. "My father was also manufacturing mattresses," Gregorio recalled, "and the mattresses were made of wool..." The object was to push the heavy wool by hand through a machine that shoved the wool into the mattresses. The wool was untreated, so the material was heavy, thick and unprocessed, which made it hard, muscle-building work.

When he was 17, Gregorio got his first summer job with an outside company, the Swift meatpacking plant. He got a job on the sixth floor where the cans were manufactured, and he worked the night shift. "It was very interesting because the cans were coming on a line, they would go through the floor to where the meat was loaded up," Gregorio recalled. "It was a very efficient process, especially for that time."

For the younger generation, life was not all hard work. During the day, "Every empty lot was used for soccer," Gregorio said. He played soccer with many friends, and on Sunday night they might all pile into the family car to take in a movie, which usually was a double feature for twenty-five cents. Mostly they watched American westerns with subtitles, featuring dashing cowboy stars like Tom Mix and Gene Autry.

Eventually the Kort family took the major step of moving from the working-class town of Berisso to La Plata, a move that reflected their growing success in the world.

And so the stage was set for two young people to catch each other's eye. One was a hardworking son of a businessman, eager to make his way in the world. The other was a determined student who took her education into her own hands at the age of five. Together, they would expand the family story to yet another new country, and bring their shared vision, insights and innovations to a new profession.

CHAPTER TWO

GOYO AND BEBA

After Gregorio and Haydee caught each other's eye, it wasn't long before they knew they wanted to be together. But before they could meet at all, they needed a matchmaker, and their matchmaker happened to be the Jewish club that their families belonged to in La Plata.

In La Plata, a prestigious university town close to Buenos Aires, Jewish clubs were the center of social life for families, especially from the 1930s through the 1950s. Between the first and second world wars, millions of eastern Europeans escaped the Nazi Third Reich to find a welcome in Argentina's capital city, making Buenos Aires home to one of the largest Jewish communities in the world. The clubs were a great source of preserving the Jewish culture and the Yiddish language, and they also opened up a new world of Latin American customs that marked many family milestones—as Gregorio and Haydee would soon find.

This particular Jewish club was familiar to Rosa and Abram Kort, as well as Jose Kantorovich. Sofia, Haydee's mother, was born in Argentina, but she came from a Jewish-Polish heritage as well. Besides bringing together people who shared a heritage and a history, the club stressed a social and intellectual atmosphere, and was a lively center for lectures, events and family parties, and get-togethers of all kinds. There were other Jewish clubs that stressed religion and were strictly Orthodox, but Gregorio and Haydee's parents were not religious so they preferred a club with a more social atmosphere. The Korts were businesspeople, and the Kantoroviches moved in the world of professional dentistry. Sofia Kantorovich was a businesswoman who had started two shops on her own. So these two hardworking families had things in common, most of all the fact that they were each raising a talented child who was determined to do something special in the world.

Their children, Gregorio and Haydee, enjoyed the club as well, and like the rest of the younger generation they stopped by for events and socializing at least two or three times a week. But first came other responsibilities. Number one was school, which for Gregorio and Haydee was strict and no-nonsense and intended to lead to a university degree. In addition to schoolwork and study, Haydee took piano lessons from a noted instructor, and she was a serious ballet student who appeared in professional productions. Gregorio was working for his parents at the furniture store and often pulling night shifts at the Swift company. On long summer afternoons, he found time to slip away and stretch his taut muscles even more on the soccer fields with his friends.

So, like most young people, Gregorio and Haydee found that life was rushing in on all sides. However, it didn't take long for each of them to realize that when they stopped in the club for a lecture or an evening dance, something new was happening.

For Haydee, it was the sight of Gregorio, the fit young man with the thoughtful and dignified air. "I liked the way he acted, the way he talked, the way he treated me with a lot of respect," she said. "I don't think I would have gone to the Jewish club if it was not for him…"

Gregorio was alert to the situation as well, and he saw something very important in the graceful young woman. "I said to myself, 'I like her,'" Gregorio recalled, adding with a smile, "I had really good taste."

At previous dances when Haydee came with her girlfriends, Gregorio would seize the opportunity to dance with her. Then came the special celebration called the quinceañera, and that changed everything.

In Latin America, the quinceañera is a grand party thrown by parents for their daughters when they reach the age of 15. Part debutante party and part coming-of-age party, the celebration (now popular in the U.S.) marks a young woman's transition from childhood to young womanhood.

So of course, when Haydee reached 15, Jose and Sofia planned a memorable quinceañera for their beautiful and talented only daughter. They invited two hundred guests to the Jewish club, and there was music, food and dancing. Every eye surely was on Haydee, as her quinceañera photos attest to this day: She was lovely and regal in her white, traditional quinceañera dress that her mother made for her, and the gown was even more striking thanks to Haydee's dancer's bearing and graceful manner.

Already a ballet dancer and pianist at 15, Haydee was often the center of attention. But on the day of her quinceañera, Haydee's attention was turned to the crowd, and she was looking for someone special.

A record player was spinning several kinds of music into the air. There was tango music, and a jazzy kind of bolero music made popular in Mexico, and the waltz. Haydee, already an accomplished ballerina, danced to classical music, and she loved the beauty of the traditional waltz.

So, when a waltz began to play and Gregorio Kort asked her to dance, well, that was pretty much *it* for both of them.

"She told me later that she liked how I squeezed her when we danced," Gregorio said, with a smile.

The quinceañera was a turning point. From then on, the 17-year-old boy and the 15-year-old girl sensed they would be together. However, because they were so young, they followed the custom of building their future through a long courtship that would last through their university years. Gregorio, who was called Goyo by his family and friends (and is to this very day), began to ask Beba (as Haydee is called) to movies, parties and events. Of course the Jewish club continued to play a big part in their courtship: "It was a case of, 'Can I pick you up to go to the club, there's going to be a nice party...'"

So the team of "Goyo and Beba" was forged, and they began to plan their life together. Each of them had already built an excellent secondary education record in their neighborhood schools. The schools were designed either all-boys or all-girls and they had strict entrance requirements. Serious learning was emphasized. "It was much more sophisticated than it is in the United States," Gregorio observed. The secondary schools were affiliated with the university, Universidad La Plata, and students were held to high standards in subjects that included history, geography, philosophy and mathematics.

In Argentina, graduate school was free, so there was no tuition burden for any young person eager to continue to higher education. However, that goal was balanced by an equally important responsibility: helping the family. Young people were expected to work and to contribute to the support of the household when necessary. Years before, as he was getting his business established, Abram Kort had set the rule that his sons had to give half their salaries to their mother. By the time their youngest son Gregorio came along the rule had eased somewhat, but he was still expected to contribute.

As for Haydee, her situation was different. By the time she was born her parents were already well to do, and they saw value in allowing their talented daughter to pursue the arts. She was achieving recognition in her ballet and piano lessons, and those pursuits were regarded as just as valuable for her future as a summer job.

Although their family backgrounds differed in some respects, in one way Gregorio and Haydee were of the same mind. The young couple was determined to complete a university education and go on to graduate school, which would lead to a profession such as law, medicine or engineering. The question was, *which* profession?

For Gregorio, the choice was easy. Even before he and Haydee began their courtship he knew he wanted to go to medical school: "I had a fantasy about how nice it would be to be a doctor, and be a resource and a consultant for the whole family, but at that time, it was pure fantasy…"

As for Haydee, "I wasn't sure that would be what I was going to do. I knew I was going to go to college and get a career of some kind. I think I became interested in medical school because I was going with Goyo, and he was going to go to medical school. Otherwise I don't think I would have done it."

The couple both applied to La Plata University Medical School and were automatically admitted. Once again, as she did at the age of five, Haydee became an educational pioneer. At five she was a standout as the very youngest student ever in the school, and when she began medical school at the age of 17, Haydee was one of only four women in a class of 150 men.

As medical school began, they continued to live with their families, but now they had a new purpose: they were in love and learning together and working toward the same goal, to become physicians. Besides, they saw a practical upside to their romance.

"We said, 'Wouldn't it be nice to study together?'" Greg recalled.

Haydee added: "And so we did, from the very first class of medical school until the end." The couple usually studied in Haydee's home, which was bigger and quieter—she had only one brother, Alberto, while Gregorio had to navigate around a family of six.

The next six years were grueling, not only with academic study, but with hands-on experience working with patients in the pediatric and geriatric wards. Gregorio explained, "It was a common joke as a medical student that when you enter medical school, you give your soul to the medical school and they don't give it back to you until you graduate. That's very close to the truth. Between classes and tests and labs and things, there was little time for anything else."

When it came to school itself, Gregorio and Haydee said they never felt a competition with each other. Instead, they shored up each other's strengths whenever necessary, which was surely a precursor to the extraordinary teamwork they developed many years later in Pueblo.

Haydee watched how her future husband approached medical school and learned from him. "He was a better student than I was," she said. "I was two years younger and I think I had a little more difficulty catching on than he did. He provided me with a lot of support until I caught up with it."

When Haydee was assigned to work with children on a pediatric ward, that practical experience was what she needed. But nothing was wasted in their relationship, even in the early days of medical school when the teenaged Haydee felt she was lagging behind. Instead of getting discouraged, the couple turned those challenges into making their relationship stronger: "I relied a lot on him and that helped us get closer," Haydee said.

$$\sim$$

During the long years when their "souls belonged to the medical school," Gregorio and Haydee continued to live with their parents while they studied together and tried to envision their future, which was pressing in on them more and more. After all, they had met and fallen in love in 1948, and now the late 1950s were closing in!

Finally, their last medical school class ended in April 1957, and they were faced with two prospects. One prospect was happy, the other, uncertain.

The happy prospect was their engagement. As was the Jewish custom, a party was arranged at the home of the groom, and about twenty people were invited from both families. Haydee remained out of sight in a room upstairs, while Gregorio asked Haydee's father for her hand in marriage. When the answer was yes, Haydee came downstairs and Gregorio presented her with a striking engagement ring. Then as is the Jewish custom, he broke a plate to signify the break from the past, and the fact that their engagement marked the beginning of a new family relationship.

The second prospect was more uncertain: How would they make their livelihood as physicians? "There was not light at the end of the tunnel about being able to get married and have a medical practice that will sustain us," Gregorio recalled. "We asked ourselves, 'What can we do?' After six years of really grinding to get our degrees, we didn't want to face many more years trying to get our practice off the ground before we got married."

In other words, they wanted to be married, but they also wanted to be married and self-sufficient, working physicians. The question was, how could they combine both goals as soon as possible? In Argentina, the road to financial stability would be a long one. Then one day as they were lamenting their choices, a doctor friend gave them a new idea:

"He told us that the American Embassy was looking for physicians to come to America and work in residency training and internships," Gregorio said. Eagerly, the young graduates sought out more information from the embassy and learned that they could each apply for a "rotating internship" that took in all the specialties, including pediatrics, geriatrics and psychiatry.

The team of Goyo and Beba went right to work—they quickly sent out one hundred letters to hospitals and medical facilities throughout the United States. They had no time to waste, either, because the application deadline was closing in, and successful applicants had to report for work on July 1, 1957.

But now they faced a problem, albeit a happy one. Goyo and Beba's wedding was scheduled for July 21, 1957, three weeks later *after* they were supposed to report for work in America.

At that point, a benevolent destiny intervened. The application committee accepted their delay, and even allowed the extra seventeen days it took to travel by ship from Buenos Aires to America.

First came the happy traditions of their wedding, including an engagement party in Gregorio's family home, complicated by exam finals. "We were very, very busy with graduating from medical school," he said, "so no sooner had we graduated than we had a very small group for the engagement party..."

Then came the wedding, or as Gregorio liked to kid, the wedding that happened three times. With their departure for America looming, they had to rush to get their civil marriage documents completed. "We couldn't wait because it takes time," Gregorio said. A short time later (the exact time frame is a blur) Gregorio and Haydee were married by the family's rabbi in a small religious ceremony attended mostly by parents and close family. It was a Jewish tradition the young couple, dressed in decorous suits (Haydee wore grey, Gregorio wore blue) were happy to fulfill to please their parents, and it included the traditional smashing of the glass, signifying the absolute finality of the marriage covenant. Finally, on July 21, came the party with between 150 and 200 guests at the hall, where Haydee donned a long wedding dress and everyone celebrated, but inevitably recognized that this was also a goodbye. To this day, it is July 21 that Haydee and Gregorio consider their wedding anniversary.

Soon after, the young couple boarded the ship, the *Rio Tunuyan,* and spent their honeymoon heading for a country and a city completely unknown to them.

In fact, the young couple had chosen their first home in America pretty much at random. "We just wrote letters," Haydee said. "We picked Nashville Memorial Hospital in Nashville, Tennessee because they seemed to be more open to the flexibility of our schedule. We weren't going to make the July 1 deadline, and they accepted that, so we decided to go to Tennessee."

After all, they had no frame of reference for weighing their decision. "We were not acquainted with the United States," Gregorio added, "so to say Kentucky is better than Nashville, or Nashville is worse than wherever, well, we didn't know!"

~

For two young people in love, the challenges were sweet and adventure loomed, and finally, after a seventeen-day sail on the stormy Atlantic, the Statue of Liberty loomed too. The young honeymooners stepped off the ship with two medical diplomas under their arms and two hundred dollars in their pockets. Waiting for them at the dock were relatives of Gregorio's mother Rosa, who were originally from Poland and now living happily in Brooklyn.

Gregorio and Haydee's newly minted American relatives took one look at the fresh young couple from Argentina and instantly proposed a change of plan: Why, oh why couldn't they stay in New York?

"They cried because we were going to Tennessee," Haydee recalled. "'No, no,' they said, 'we will find you something in New York! You must stay here with us!'"

"But we have a contract, we must report for work in Nashville," Gregorio protested.

The relatives were heartbroken. In addition to that tender and well-meaning family argument, a few other problems surfaced during their one-week stay in Brooklyn. Most of all, the relatives were appalled at Gregorio and Haydee's decision to begin their careers in America's Deep South, which not only promoted black segregation but was known for its virulent anti-Semitism.

"They were upset that we were going to the terrible South where they don't like anybody," Gregorio said. "They couldn't believe it."

Haydee recalled their passionate arguments. "They said, 'Don't you know Tennessee is a horrible place, especially for Jewish people? You are going to be living with racists there!'"

Goyo and Haydee were firm. They were going to report for work as they promised. "Well, you will have to take a bus to Tennessee," their crushed relatives replied. The young couple was ready for anything, and a bus ride certainly didn't seem out of the ordinary, at least not then.

Another problem was language, though that problem was more amusing than disturbing. "We arrived as typical immigrants," Gregorio said. "Here we are, coming off the boat and we thought that we knew English, but very quickly we learned that we didn't know that much…"

"In Argentina," Haydee explained, "we learned British English, but when we got to New York and Brooklyn, British English wasn't of any use because in New York they didn't understand most of it."

Equally puzzling to Gregorio and Haydee were the hard edges of their relatives' Brooklynese accent. And when they encountered the southern drawl, even more of what they *thought* they knew about English went out the window too.

With a grin, Gregorio recalled that as a hardworking youngster in his parents' furniture store in Berisso, he dealt with customers from all over the world, and the store was always filled with the sounds of many languages colliding over one another. He thought he had heard it all. Then he had to let go of the British English he had learned in school and learn to understand Brooklynese, and after that, somehow figure out the southern drawl. This strange language, English, was something else!

"I thought I knew English," Gregorio said. "Then what do I do? I go to a country where I have to learn the same language all over again!"

~

Their farewell at the New York City bus station was plunged in gloom. The relatives were still heartbroken and openly weeping. It was inconceivable that Gregorio and Haydee, this vibrant young couple who represented the next generation of their family, would not be staying with them in New York, but going to Tennessee, a backward state, perhaps even a dangerous one.

In the chaos of the bumping and jostling bus station crowd, Gregorio and Haydee tried to comfort their weeping relatives and at the same time listen for their bus announcement to Nashville. In the hurly-burly of the moment all the departure announcements sounded the same, like rapid-fire barking. "If somebody was speaking English slowly, to our face, we could understand," Gregorio recalled. "But all the announcements sounded like gibberish. We didn't want to miss our stop for Nashville. I mean, we were pretty anxious about it!"

As the bus lurched out of Brooklyn and headed for the highway, the young couple sat rigid and tense in their seats. At each of the next two or three stops, the driver made an announcement that sounded like more gibberish. The tension was growing—they couldn't miss their stop! Finally, and very calmly, Haydee whispered to her young husband, "Go up and ask the driver how much farther to Nashville, or did we miss it?'

So Gregorio went up to the driver and asked, "Sir, how much farther to Nashville, or did we miss the stop?"

Today both Gregorio and Haydee laugh as they remember the bus driver's gasps of astonishment: "Not only didn't you miss it, you have two more days on the bus!"

It was their first lesson in American geography. "We thought Nashville was a couple of hours away from New York," Gregorio said, chuckling.

The bus ride to Nashville was just the opening chapter in a series of challenges that faced the team of Goyo and Beba in the "Deep South." Looking back more than fifty years later, Haydee recalled the depressing living conditions when they first arrived.

"It wasn't the life that you'd really wish for yourself when you were just married," she said. "It was not the American dream."

CHAPTER THREE

"WHAT DID WE GET OURSELVES INTO?"

While Gregorio and Haydee were chugging by bus across America from New York to Tennessee with two hundred dollars in their pocket and two medical diplomas in hand, their family back in Argentina was worrying over one big unanswered question: "When are you coming home?" Their hope was that after a year of internship the young couple would return to Argentina.

In Goyo and Beba's eyes, the future was much less settled. What would they find in Nashville? They did not know, but like all young people, they could not imagine a future as anything less than sweet, because they were together. Whatever challenges were ahead they would explore them as a team, as Goyo and Beba. Nevertheless, they felt a deep obligation to their parents who had so lovingly supported their plans, even though it required the heavy sacrifice to let them go.

To pay for their international adventure, Goyo and Beba raised funds by doing public-health work, such as giving injections and immunizations. Once in America, their long hours were not over. The trip they thought would be a few hours took three days. They arrived with aching bones and heavy eyes, but that was only the beginning of their challenges.

Gregorio and Haydee had won separate internships at Nashville Memorial Hospital. Each of those awards came with a promise of room and board on the hospital grounds, plus a salary of $125 a month (the equivalent of about $1,100 a month in 2018).

But their hopes of enjoying their USA adventure together, as a married couple, soon evaporated for a very basic reason: The young newlyweds weren't allowed to live together! Interns were expected to live on the hospital grounds, which meant Gregorio was assigned a room with two male interns and Haydee was paired with a female intern from Korea.

Not for the last time, Haydee thought, "What did we get ourselves into?"

With a smile, Gregorio agreed: "It was an awakening."

In another way, the closeness to the hospital was good, because the schedule was brutal. They were on call twenty-four hours a day. Their first assignment was in the pediatric ward, where they were the only two interns assisting the staff and physicians. Haydee was assigned to work from 7:00 a.m. to 11:00 at night, and the next morning it was Gregorio's turn. Their entire lives were spent on the hospital grounds. Even their meals were in the hospital cafeteria. Laughing, Haydee said that in addition to the work pressures, "Those meals were terrible!"

All in all, this was not the way Goyo and Beba expected to start their professional careers. Most important, they needed to live together. They needed each other's support, and they needed a life away from the hospital. But how could they make that point to their boss? They were worried that their English was still too tentative to express themselves effectively.

Carefully and laboriously, they rehearsed in English what they wanted to say. But in the end, standing before the hospital administrator, their plea was simple and came right from their hearts.

"We are just married, and we need each other!" Gregorio said. "You have to do something because we cannot continue like this!"

The administrator made them wait a week while he considered their case. Finally, he offered a grudging solution: "If you can find a room to rent that's within ten or fifteen minutes of the hospital, even though you will be on call, we will allow you to leave the grounds."

At first, Goyo and Beba were overjoyed at the opportunity. It didn't take long for them to realize their room and board challenges had just begun.

First of all, the young newlyweds had a small area to choose from because their accommodations had to be within fifteen minutes of the hospital, and the hospital itself was in a rundown and segregated area of town. The area reflected the deeply divided South of the late 1950s where racism was rampant, and where disadvantaged African Americans were shunted off into ghettos with their own language and customs. For the third or fourth time, Haydee said, "We were learning English all over again."

Later, they found that to live so closely with Americans gave them insight that was invaluable. Many of their patients were black, and to be immersed themselves in black southern culture in their own neighborhood gave Gregorio and Haydee an understanding of their patients that was unique. Plus, in a very practical way, it helped the Spanish-speaking couple "learn English" all over again, as they grew familiar with the unfamiliar cadences of American English as spoken in the South.

Far more difficult to conquer was their living situation itself.

The only accommodation they could find was a room in a house that they shared with a Korean family of seven.

"It was a block away so we could get there in fifteen minutes," Haydee said, "but we shared it with a family of five kids. All we had was a room, and to get to our room we had to step over the kids watching TV. Our room was so small, and there were no closets, nothing! Just a room filled with boxes of our things. We had to share a bathroom with the whole family, including the five kids!"

One bright spot was the rent, which was only thirty dollars a month. With salaries of $125 a month each, Gregorio and Haydee felt that, money-wise, they were starting out pretty well. But that only made them more determined to pay back the precious gift of two hundred dollars they had carried with them from Argentina.

Financial independence was a matter of honor, as Gregorio explained: "Basically the two of us didn't want to depend financially on our parents because we felt we were already betraying them by leaving the country."

"They weren't crazy about it," added Haydee. "My parents were very upset."

The two hundred dollars had been a gift from Gregorio's uncle Roberto Turkenich. Shortly before they left, he took the young couple into his bedroom where he handed them the precious travel funds. "You can't go without money," he said. "Now you have this money. Pay us back whenever you have a chance."

Gregorio and Haydee made that chance happen almost immediately. "We were making $125 a month each, and we had no place to spend it," Haydee pointed out. "So we were able to return his money almost right away."

They were in love and financially solvent, but beyond that, their new life in America was proving to be pretty bleak.

~

Added to their challenges was the nagging problem of how to soothe their parents' worries. "There were no telephones or email so the letters we sent were fantasy," Gregorio said. "We didn't tell them we had to live in those conditions and that we had to work every other day for eleven hours straight..."

"Those letters had very little to do with reality," Haydee agreed. "We were telling them that we love our jobs. Everything is hunky dory!"

"No use telling them otherwise," Gregorio said.

Haydee knew that her parents were especially crushed to lose their only daughter and new son-in-law, even if it was only for the space of one year. "My parents were not happy at all that we came," she said. "And we didn't want to disappoint them even further by telling them what we were going through."

Both families clung to what they believed was the one bright spot: After a year of internship, the young couple would be back in Argentina.

Then things began to happen.

One of the attending physicians, Dr. Lee, took an interest in the young Argentine couple and began to mentor them informally. Dr. Lee was a pediatrician, but he had a special interest in psychiatry, a specialty which neither Gregorio nor Haydee had considered. Thanks to Dr. Lee, their interest was piqued. Almost on cue, another physician engrossed by psychiatry stepped into their lives.

Dr. Bustos was a physician, also from Argentina, who in fact had gone to medical school with Gregorio and Haydee. Now that he was in America, he was determined to enter the field of psychiatry.

Dr. Bustos told the young Korts they should consider a residency in psychiatry. To the couple, the idea was intriguing, and different enough to lift their spirits from their dreary beginnings. "We felt, 'What the heck? Let's do it!'" Gregorio said. "We will be together and we can support each other."

So, that's when they moved to a psychiatric residency program. The decision would not only change their lives, but would impact the field of psychiatry and the development of mental health policies across the USA.

∼

Now events were moving quickly. Dr. Bustos, their Argentine colleague, was moving to Bolivar, Tennessee, where he was set to begin his psychiatric residency at the Western State Hospital. At his urging, Gregorio and Haydee applied, and both were accepted into the program at Western State Hospital.

One good thing rolled into another, and pretty soon a floodgate of good things was kicked open. The hospital in Bolivar offered Gregorio and Haydee a two-bedroom apartment and a monthly food stipend of one hundred dollars, plus a monthly salary for each of $425, which quadrupled their salary in Nashville.

No more exhausting hospital rotations, fifteen-minute dashes to the hospital, or stepping over five children and unpacked boxes to get to the bathroom!

Besides that, the hospital in Bolivar pulled out the red carpet for Gregorio and Haydee. "We were very welcomed," Gregorio said. "The interview was an easy thing because they said to us, 'Do you agree to come? Good! You're hired.'"

In fact, he added, "We got an incredible promotion."

Meanwhile, Haydee had no problem revising her thoughts about going back to Argentina. She, like Gregorio, was becoming very happy in their new country. But she was still troubled to realize that her parents' worst fears were coming true. Their daughter and son-in-law's adventure in the USA was turning out to have "forever" written all over it. "My parents were right," she said. "We were beginning to get acquainted with things, we were getting used to the language, the hospital work was good, we liked where we were living, and the administration liked us a lot. They took us under their wing and they really went out of their way to welcome us."

Nevertheless, Goyo and Beba were about to learn there was another side to "southern hospitality" that was deeply troubling.

The first inkling of division was the friendly list of "do's and don'ts" laid out for Gregorio and Haydee by the staff and administration.

This was a transition era that separated the 1950s from what would become the more racially enlightened 1960s. While integration was being attempted in the South, segregation was deeply entrenched, and the hospital staff made sure the newly arrived couple from Argentina understood the rules which governed daily life in the South: Don't forget there are black bathrooms and white bathrooms. And under no circumstances can a black family sit in the same waiting room as a white family.

There was this too: "Never accept an invitation to a black person's home or you will be labeled a n— lover."

The ugly "rules" were laid out in an amiable, "we want you to know this is how we do things" kind of way, but the Korts were appalled. They had not been raised like this, and the customs felt depressing and sad.

"This was the culture and feelings that permeated everything," Gregorio said. "For example, the director of the hospital and many of the staff psychiatrists were very rude when they interviewed a black patient. The assistant superintendent would address a black patient aggressively: 'You ——, tell me the truth!'

"They never called a black patient 'Mister' or 'Missus,'" Haydee said. "We had to go along with it because there was no other choice. It was the way things were done. We were already there, these were our bosses, and that's the way they dealt with things."

Gregorio was assigned to the black wards, while Haydee was immediately assigned to the admission ward, which was considered a prize assignment because those patients were white. Why the difference in their assignments? There may have been the cultural prejudice that Haydee, as a white woman, should be "protected" from contact with blacks. In any case, the doctor in charge took Haydee under his wing. "He said he would make a point to teach me everything that I needed to know."

Gregorio has an additional explanation for why Haydee was singled out. He said she was immediately identified as a resident whom everyone wanted to mentor and work with. Meanwhile, he was assigned to a ward of female African Americans, where he quickly discovered the special qualities of his patients. "I was very happy working with my black ladies," he said. In fact, he was so taken with their life stories and deep spirituality that he would

44

steal back to the ward after he had made his rounds, just to be around them and learn from them.

"They were very interesting ladies," Gregorio said. "What I would do, is go in the morning and do my work, and then after the rounds and the medications in the afternoon I would go back to the ward, which I didn't have to do, and I would sit down in the circle with them and listen to them sing spirituals."

Sitting quietly to the side, Gregorio noticed something that was deeply moving.

"It was amazing that these patients didn't know each other, but they immediately were singing in harmony!" he said. "That was the first time I heard the song, 'He's got the whole world in His hands.' I loved the spirituals they sang."

Together, Gregorio and Haydee were seeing the worst and the best of the southern culture. As for the black patients, they appreciated the fact the two "Dr. Korts" treated them with dignity and respect. Their reputation quickly grew that they were very good to the black patients. "They liked us," Gregorio said. As for changing the harsh segregation of the hospital, "It was obvious to us that there was no use challenging what was an ingrained culture. "

The black patients, along with their families, welcomed Gregorio and Haydee. "The feeling was, even though we were white, somebody cared about them," Gregorio said. "I think that fulfilled a lot of what we wanted to do, to be all-caring to our patients. We were fantasizing what it could be if we could change the other things, but the best we could do was to take good care of them."

Something else was becoming clear, Gregorio added: "There was no question that we liked psychiatry, and we were good."

~

Their professional lives were beginning to gel, and soon Gregorio and Haydee had a new and personal reason for their happiness.

"I became pregnant with our son while we were in Bolivar in 1959," Haydee said. "Our son Marcelo was born in Memphis, and things were beginning to really click in our lives. Even though the practice wasn't ideal, we knew we were going to continue to do psychiatry, but in a more modern setting. But we knew we had to go through that experience in order to get to the next one."

Meanwhile, they were enjoying parenthood and family life.

Family life was extremely important to Goyo and Beba; in fact, in future years they arranged their hospital schedules so they could always be home at five o'clock to spend the dinner hour and the rest of the evening with their children. In fact, "Home by Five!" became a rallying cry for their family life.

Marcelo Eduardo (born in 1959) and Gabriela Jennifer (born in 1963) were planned for and welcomed. Haydee found it easy to get pregnant ("When we decided to get pregnant, we got pregnant").

Haydee found working and pregnancy went together well. In Bolivar before Marcelo was born, "I was working in a privileged area, a controlled and quiet environment where no one was disturbed or upset," she said. Her job was in the admissions office, far from the crowded conditions and often raw emotions that Gregorio saw in the wards. Happily, the couple each enjoyed their own environments. Gregorio loved working with patients one on one, while Haydee was finding administrative challenges equally fulfilling.

Together, they shared a strong and affectionate love for their firstborn child.

"I found being a father very exciting," Gregorio said. "It gave us another dimension to our life, to be away from dealing with patients and staff and the culture and so on. This was *ours.*"

As for motherhood, "It's hard to describe, the feeling, the emotion when you hold your first child," Haydee said. "The only problem I had was, it took twenty-four hours to deliver the baby! But after that, there was nothing greater in the world than that baby; nothing more special."

They named their son Marcelo, because it was a Spanish name they liked, and because they wanted their family to have a strong connection to their heritage. Haydee explained, "Being psychiatrists and thinking about the subconscious, we wanted our children to have Hispanic names."

Marcelo's birth was the cause of another joy: Haydee's mother, Sofia, came from Argentina to be there shortly after the baby's birth. "She was so excited to come and help me take care of the baby and be a full-time grandma," Haydee recalled.

"I think it also gave us additional focus to our life to have her with us," Gregorio said. "We were dealing with issues at work and the whole cultural thing of being in the South. So to have Haydee's mother there helped us enjoy the time without worrying about anything, and just being with our son."

Although southern customs were often cruel when it came to race, when it came to family and motherhood, sweet southern hospitality ruled.

"We were very lucky that all the wives of the physicians of the hospital were extremely supportive of Haydee," Gregorio recalled.

"They acted like surrogate mothers around Marcelo, and gave him incredible birthday gifts. It's important to understand this about dealing with people, even when you're offended by some of their cultural thinking, it's not that they don't have a kind heart when they want to."

Haydee's mother fit right into the new family, which now included the nanny, Vaserine.

"They got along perfectly," Haydee said. "My mother concentrated on the baby and Vaserine concentrated on the house and all the things around the baby. They divided up the chores and got along just fine."

Vaserine was a very special person in the Kort household, although her presence would eventually bring the southern culture into an even sharper and more uncomfortable focus.

"When the baby is born, you will need a mammy," came word from the hospital administration. Without further ado, the assistant superintendent of the hospital presented Haydee and Gregorio with a list of recommended names of black ladies whose job was to work for a white family to help raise their children; these women represented that legendary southern icon known as a "mammy."

By that time, the Korts were treasured employees, and the administration wanted to find them the best "mammy" possible. "I'll recommend you to the best one that has ever taken care of kids," the assistant superintendent promised.

In fact, Vaserine *was* the best. She came with glowing recommendations from families, and her recommendations included the names of every one of the children she had ever raised. Vaserine, who was in her forties, was known to be especially skilled at raising children from their babyhood. Quickly, Vaserine became a trusted and beloved person in the Kort family.

Shortly after she began working for the family, the assistant superintendent called Gregorio into his office. Gregorio recalled the scene. "The assistant superintendent said, 'I love you guys and I know what you're going through because you only have one bathroom."

The young father reeled back in shock. What the assistant superintendent was saying—and saying in a completely friendly and "it's us against them" kind of way—was that Vaserine wasn't good enough to use the family bathroom! Worse was the fact that the assistant superintendent was so blinded to his own racism that he assumed Gregorio and Haydee would completely agree with him.

"Don't worry," the assistant superintendent said, "I'll get maintenance to build an outhouse in the back of your apartment."

The conversation left Gregorio nearly speechless. "'Let me think about it,'" I said. "But that was the steamroller we needed to start looking for a job. We knew we couldn't win that battle."

Haydee added, "We couldn't win it and we weren't about to get into it with them. We knew there was no way."

Unknown to the assistant superintendent, his well-intentioned but inhumane gesture helped to send Gregorio and Haydee's future in a new direction. Sadly, the impact fell on the wonderful relationship they had built with Vaserine. In the year she worked for them, she achieved the status of close family.

Said Haydee, "She was a dear lady, she took care of our son while we worked hard all day, and she would do anything for him...in the meantime, we didn't follow up with the assistant superintendent about putting in another bathroom, and after that, he didn't approach us about it again."

To this day, Gregorio and Haydee are left with sweet memories of Vaserine, who loved the family, and especially Marcelo, very deeply. Said Haydee, "She loved that baby like one of her own. It was really wonderful."

Especially interesting was to watch how her care and concern for the little boy often took on a cultural flavor. For instance, Vaserine begged Haydee not to cut Marcelo's hair for his first year because it would compromise his development.

"Because we respected her and that was how she felt, we did what she asked, and didn't cut Marcelo's hair," Haydee recalled. "Then on his first birthday, we came home from work to find his hair all cut up in different directions—Vaserine was true to her word, he was now a year old and he had to have his hair cut!"

Smiling at the memory, Gregorio added, "She wanted to surprise us by doing it before we came home."

Vaserine was heartbroken when she learned the family was leaving Tennessee, and Gregorio and Haydee were equally sad to leave the unforgettable Vaserine. But they knew they were being called to someplace new.

Their adventure in America's Deep South was over.

CHAPTER FOUR

"WE WANT TO DO THIS FOREVER"

Life in America's Deep South clarified many important things for Gregorio and Haydee Kort. One of them was to answer the question: "Should we *stay* in the South?" That answer was easy, and their response was united: "We have to get out of this place." They were disturbed by the racism of the era, the lack of empathy toward patients, and the cultural resistance to innovation.

In other ways, however, life in the South in the late 1950s was a positive experience whose effects radiated through the rest of their lives. It was in Tennessee that "the two Dr. Korts" recognized their skills and the value they brought to the field of mental health and the psychiatric profession. And away from work, Goyo and Beba were building a life all their own. After all, it was in Memphis that their son Marcelo was born, and it was in the South that the young family was able to establish their first real home.

Even as their personal and professional lives grew happier, the question of remaining in the United States was stabbing at their consciences. Until 1959 when the matter was finally resolved, they knew their parents were hoping against hope they would eventually return to Argentina. Reluctantly, Gregorio and Haydee delayed raising the issue with their families, even though their own minds and hearts were becoming settled: They wanted to make their home in America.

As their way forward became clearer, so did the distress they felt for their parents' sake. "We knew it would upset them," Haydee said, and Gregorio agreed. "We didn't want to lie, but we didn't want to discuss it either," he said.

Perhaps delaying the conversation would soften the blow? The young couple hoped so. In the meantime, they explained to their parents that it would greatly benefit their future careers if they stayed in America long enough to find jobs on their own merits, not as young resident physicians (as they were in Nashville and Bolivar) but as established psychiatrists.

That was the argument they put to their parents, anyway, and it was true, as far as it went. While the South would never be their permanent home, they were energized by their work and felt a growing self-confidence that they had something to offer the psychiatric profession and its rapidly changing landscape.

The question was, where could they contribute best?

In fact, the future was opening up for young professionals with innovative ideas like Gregorio and Haydee. They had the good fortune to begin their psychiatric careers at a historic moment for the profession, and at a time which was considered no less than "the second revolution" in the treatment of the mentally ill.

The first revolution happened in the 1880s when a fiery activist, Dorothea Dix, succeeded in her campaign to require every state in the USA to establish a state-run institution for the mentally ill. Until then, mentally ill individuals were left to shift for themselves, which often meant living a homeless "street" existence, or hidden away as a family's shameful secret. For the next 75 years, the establishment of state-run institutions was a compassionate improvement that provided food and shelter to patients but no actual treatment of their illnesses.

The second revolution came in the mid-1950s with the arrival of powerful drugs which marked the first *medical* treatment of psychiatric illnesses. This pharmaceutical breakthrough was able to stabilize, and many times halt, the course of psychiatric illnesses, allowing countless sufferers to emerge from the shadows and live in the world again.

Thorazine, the first of the anti-psychotic drugs, came to market in 1955. Thorazine was the first drug specifically designed to address psychotic symptoms and schizophrenia, including hallucinations and paranoia. With the help of Thorazine and similar drug therapies, many patients could reenter society, rejoin their families, find careers, and become full and functioning citizens. Even during periods of hospitalization (whether their stays were temporary or long term), patients who were treated with these anti-psychotic drugs were able to function far better than ever before, and this fact alone required new and individualized approaches to their care.

For Gregorio and Haydee, poised on the threshold of their careers, this second revolution offered exciting opportunities that perfectly fit their talents and inclinations. Even tucked away in a small hospital in Bolivar, Tennessee, they recognized this revolution in psychiatric care had the potential to truly help human beings *if it was used effectively.* Together, the two Drs. Kort tackled the question: "We debated in our minds how this could be done. We can medicate patients and send them home because they are not hallucinating anymore. But is that life? Don't we have something else to offer?"

Young, eager and still relatively inexperienced, Gregorio and Haydee nevertheless had the insight to recognize that the second revolution was much more than a pharmaceutical triumph—it required new ways of interacting with patients and developing individualized care. Led by skilled and knowledgeable staff, the new approach meant that many patients could be helped now on an outpatient basis, while others could continue to live in a freer institutional setting and still develop meaningful lives.

One of their first major insights was to recognize the potential uses of psychotherapy, which treats the psychological rather than the medical roots of mental illness. The two Drs. Kort saw that this sector of the mental health field was grossly underdeveloped. In response, they envisioned a central role for psychotherapy groups which, in concert with medications, would give patients access to behavioral solutions and supportive help from their fellow patients.

"We wanted to provide a more complete treatment that worked with real psychotherapy techniques as well as medications," Haydee explained. "And we wanted to be more in charge."

In charge? Yes, the two young resident psychiatrists felt a growing confidence and awareness in their own abilities, and that led to a natural and life-changing decision about their own future. As Haydee put it, "We had come to like this specialty very much, and we decided we want to do this forever."

~

All the while, they were gaining in experience and learning from their patients. Some of the lessons they learned were peculiar to living in the South. Gregorio recalled one especially unforgettable case.

He was edified to note that one of his patients, a black woman, was visited every first Sunday of the month by a kindly and polite white man. Given the place and times, this was highly unusual. "The man would come up and talk to me and say, 'Please let me know when she's ready to go home and I'll come and get her.' I started commenting to the other staff, 'What a kind and generous man! He doesn't miss a Sunday, and he wants to come and pick her up!'"

Gregorio noticed that the staff were looking at each other as if debating whether to tell him something. Finally, one of them spoke up. "He is a plantation owner," the attendant explained. "This girl comes from his plantation and he wants to make sure she goes back there. If she is released into her family's care, that news will get back to the plantation and all his other black workers will use the same ruse, come to the hospital for medications, and then take off!"

Today, Gregorio smiles ruefully at his youthful naivety, but the incident also highlighted the entrenched ideas of that time and place: "There was no empathy towards the mentally ill." There was no protection for them, either, especially for patients like the woman who worked on a plantation and came from a depressed socio-economic background. Their mental illnesses had left them without social skills or career prospects, and they were often at the mercy of others.

Together, said Gregorio, he and Haydee felt an urgency to change things. "We saw a need to do something about how we are taking care of the mentally ill!"

The young physicians also recognized that their insights could never be realized if they remained where they were. "We saw there was no future there," Haydee said, "but we knew the administrators liked us a lot, so we dealt with it as best we could."

Quietly, on their own time, Goyo and Beba began to send out job inquiries to hospitals and institutions around the country. Nor did they let their relative inexperience discourage them from applying to the very best, including the world-renowned Mayo Clinic in Rochester, Minnesota.

But it was a reply from one state away from Minnesota that caught their interest and set the course of their future.

A hospital in Clarinda, Iowa, was interested.

~

It was not just the Korts' medical credentials that caught the attention of the medical director of the Iowa State Hospital.

Dr. Luis Garcia-Bunuel was a Spanish-speaking native of Spain, and his interesting background included the fact that he was the nephew of the famed movie director Luis Bunuel. In addition to sharing Gregorio and Haydee's native language and Latin and Hispanic heritage, Dr. Garcia (as he was called) shared their energy and enthusiasm for bringing fresh and innovative ideas to the field of psychiatry and mental health.

Perhaps Uncle Luis's creativity had passed on to Dr. Garcia, only to surface in a different profession? In any case, in an unlikely setting, tucked between a ninety-mile stretch of cornfields between Omaha and southeastern Iowa, Dr. Garcia was implementing an exciting and creative new way of looking at mental illness. His fresh ideas would turn the second revolution from a historic moment to a national movement, and its birthplace would be Clarinda, Iowa.

Now, to his surprise, Dr. Garcia was getting an extra boost to accomplish his dream. Out of nowhere and from an equally unlikely setting in Tennessee, he received a job inquiry from two Spanish-speaking emigres like himself who shared his vision: Dr. Gregorio Kort and Dr. Haydee Kort.

The three met, and speaking in their native Spanish, Dr. Garcia laid out his inspirational plan with energy and zest, driving home the message that he needed the two Drs. Kort to join him. Together, they could transform the field of mental health! Recalling their first meeting years later, Gregorio and Haydee chuckled at the memory of Dr. Garcia's infectious enthusiasm and agreed, "Yes, it was like a sales pitch!"

The Clarinda Plan, as it came to be nationally known, called for a fundamental reorganization of the mental health system that emphasized both individual support *and* community support for each patient.

Until then, the standard practice in mental hospitals was to put patients in arbitrary ward groupings based on their diagnoses or on their assigned tasks, such as their work in the laundry or kitchen. Patients had little in common with each other otherwise, and this artificial categorization reinforced their isolation. The staff was centralized and overseen by a powerful administrator (for example, the director of nursing), who governed the system from an impersonal and bureaucratic distance.

This status quo was shattered by the explosive energy of Dr. Garcia's dazzling new ideas. He believed patients should be living together in their own wards where they shared cultures and geographic backgrounds, and benefitted from the healing power of familiarity and sense of community.

He also believed that each reorganized ward should have its own set of professional support that consisted of a team leader and a focused, well-trained staff that included psychologists, recreational therapists and social workers. Again, the goal was to create smaller, more personalized wards where patients received both individual support *and* group support.

Dr. Garcia called his plan "Internal Geographic Decentralization." The ponderous language was deceptive; packed inside the title's heavy word-baggage was a fresh, flexible, hands-on system for treating mental illness, no less than a revolution within the second revolution.

Dr. Garcia's "sales pitch" was just what Gregorio and Haydee were waiting for. Yes, they wanted to be there to help him light the torch.

~

One of the strongest and happiest things about Gregorio's and Haydee's relationship has been their lifelong appreciation of and support for each other's skills. Like the pillars of a strong foundation, their talents have always been independent of each other but complementary and equally distributed. Throughout their active careers, this harmony of mind and heart meant that neither one ever felt competition with the other. Gregorio was intrigued and energized by working directly with patients, while Haydee was drawn to the executive skills necessary to run a hospital administration.

For Dr. Garcia-Bunuel, the professional independence and synergy of this young couple were like finding a treasure he didn't know he had been searching for. In Gregorio and Haydee he recognized an array of skills that would perfectly complement his vision of a restructured mental health system. No question, he had enough ideas and innovations to use *all* their talents.

He assigned Haydee, not yet 30 years old, to be Team Leader, a far-reaching responsibility that required excellent judgment and administrative skills.

In Gregorio, Dr. Garcia had found a psychiatrist with an instinctive understanding of individual patient behavior, whose natural calling was clinical work. Gregorio was energized by treating patients one on one, and his insights and intuition into each patient's needs fit perfectly with Bunuel's fresh and individualized approach to patients.

This was the core of Dr. Garcia's team. Now, what was the game plan?

"Well, he knew what he wanted to do," Gregorio said, adding with a grin, "but at the same time, he didn't have any more idea than the man in the moon how the team was going to discharge its responsibilities!"

At least this exciting new approach had made one thing clear, said Haydee: "We knew we wanted to do psychiatry for the rest of our lives."

CHAPTER FIVE

THE CLARINDA PLAN

When Gregorio and Haydee Kort rolled up to the grounds of the Clarinda Mental Health Institute in July 1960, little Marcelo was tucked in the back seat of their 1954 Oldsmobile, and his father and mother were in the exhilarating position of being young, talented, and about to take a life-changing step in their professional field.

Their new home, Clarinda, Iowa, was the birthplace of the Clarinda Plan, a groundbreaking way to organize mental health hospitals, and a fitting third act in the saga of two revolutions.

The first revolution was the establishing of state mental health hospitals in 1888, and the second, in 1955, was the discovery of powerful drug therapies that opened up new freedoms and possibilities for treating the mentally ill.

Now, in their new jobs, Gregorio and Haydee were tasked with bringing to life a movement that could complete the revolutionary process. The Clarinda Plan amounted to no less than replacing the entrenched system of management and patient care that became the national norm when the first state mental hospitals were founded in the late 1880s.

The introduction of anti-psychotic drugs in the mid-1950s had opened up untold new possibilities of freedom to patients. But at the time when Gregorio and Haydee arrived on the scene only a few years later, this freedom was still blocked by an old, established bureaucratic system that existed in the mental health profession at large. Patients were still regimented and treated impersonally, even though the new drugs made many of them individually capable of taking on new opportunities, both in the institutional setting and in the outside world.

A new system was needed. That's what Gregorio and Haydee's enthusiastic new boss, Dr. Luis Garcia-Bunuel, wanted to do—he wanted to unlock all the potential freedoms possible for patients who were being greatly helped by the new drug therapies.

He had complete confidence that his two new employees, the two Drs. Kort, could do the job, and his marching orders were clear:

"It's all yours," Haydee recalled him saying. "We don't have pre-conceived notions. Do whatever you can, and do the best you can."

With the endorsement of their new boss, Gregorio, 31, and Haydee, just 29, vaulted to the highest responsibilities of their pro-fession. They had been in the United States less than five years, and their new jobs were paying each of them $19,000 a year. In 2018 dollars, that amounts to a $157,000 annual salary for each Dr Kort.

"Yes, we were doing well," Gregorio agreed. But along with those heady salaries came a workload and responsibilities to match.

If the young psychiatrists ever doubted the huge task they faced to effect meaningful change, it would have been dispelled by the first sight of the hospital itself.

To this day, the campus of the old Clarinda Mental Health

Institute, with its dignified red-brick buildings and manicured lawns, radiates order, decorum, and an immovable status quo. A long rolling drive still cuts through the stately, tree-lined landscape to the administration building, whose landmark is a soaring clock tower.

The clock is long gone from the tower, and so is the original purpose of the Clarinda campus. Today it houses an addiction center. When the massive, ornate buildings were built they were designed to be, for the mentally ill, "ideal sanctuaries," to use a phrase of that long-gone era. To closet away suffering people in a secure setting was considered the "ideal" solution for helping them.

The new Clarinda Plan rejected the solution of an ideal sanctuary. Instead, it stressed a system where patients could make their best lives possible in the real world.

That was the vision anyway. But like all movements charged with revolutionary ideas, the Clarinda Plan could not plant its flag without a power struggle.

～

Veteran moviegoers will recall films where the plot turns on a visit to the "mental institution." Earlier films, like *Now, Voyager*, featured mental institutions as huge, imposing mansions, with solemn nurses in starched white uniforms and winged caps gliding down shadowed halls, and patients being escorted to supervised visits on a lush lawn. Later films, like *One Flew Over the Cuckoo's Nest*, exposed the bleak wards and staff dictatorships that infect an institutional system when it is decomposing.

In a sense, Gregorio and Haydee could see elements of both clichés when they arrived at the Clarinda Mental Health Institute in July 1961.

No question, the physical surroundings were serene, even elegant. To this day, the Clarinda buildings have preserved the wide, gracious staircases with burnished inlaid carvings, and the cozy dining and visiting areas of the past. Tall windows are still covered by exquisite lace curtains which patients created themselves long ago. This was the environment which institutions around the country were duplicating; it was an effort to give human beings burdened by mental suffering at least the illusion of stability and peace.

This kind of "custodial care" was cutting edge for its time. Yes, patients received good meals, clean beds, and work projects to occupy themselves. However, behind the scenes things looked different. Mental health institutions ran on a hierarchy of power that was designed to put great gulfs of distance between administration, staff, and patients. The Director of Nursing was a powerful central figure who, from her sturdy oak desk in the administration building, ran a huge nursing staff that animated the life of the wards. As for the patients, before the Thorazine revolution arrived to open the prison cells of their minds, many patients lived in the wards for decades, if not their whole lives. Over time, as patient populations became overburdened and swelled beyond their original capacity, many institutions lost their direction and humanity. The outer buildings, designed to be beautiful and serene, often hid inner wards that were chaotic, ugly, and overcrowded. Most people are aware of the shocking headlines and news stories told about neglected patients who lined the hallways of such institutions, forgotten by their families, stripped of basic care, bereft of dignity and hope.

Vestiges of this old, overburdened system were still very much in place when Gregorio and Haydee arrived, and they felt this human tragedy acutely.

"It was a place to 'put people,'" said Haydee. "Families couldn't care for them, so the institutions became a place to dump them, to just leave them there…"

Over the decades, as the patient rosters grew so did the bureaucracy. It was this outmoded and non-empathetic system that Dr. Garcia wanted Gregorio and Haydee to help him break up.

On a basic level, everything had to be reorganized. Dr. Garcia described this phase of the movement as Internal Geographic Decentralization. Despite the stiff language, his idea was visionary and humane. It called for transferring the institution's power from a few directors at the top, to individual teams of skilled professionals and staff who worked one on one with individual wards of patients.

The wards themselves would be reorganized too, into a more natural grouping of patients who shared hometown backgrounds, or at least came from the same geographical area of the state. Shared memories, and the comforting knowledge of living with folks from one's own county and town, were believed to have powerful therapeutic value.

The reorganization, when accomplished in total, was the essence of the Clarinda Plan.

∾

As Gregorio and Haydee observed upon their arrival, the first flaw in the old system was the impersonal way patients were grouped. Traditionally, the patient wards were organized around a patient's work assignment. So, for instance, patients who worked in Clarinda's massive laundry (a huge enterprise, given the needs of two thousand patients) all lived in the same ward. Likewise, patients who tended Clarinda's nearby farmland bunked together in the same ward. And so it went. Patients were assigned to work or daily tasks, and that assignment largely determined their ward grouping.

This grouping system may have been reasonable and efficient in the late 1880s, but by the mid-twentieth century it had become an isolating force. Beyond their daily tasks, patients had nothing in common. They had no shared backgrounds or sense of a common history or community life.

When it came to staffing, isolation was the rule of the day, too. Power flowed from the heights, starting with the superintendent and the director of nursing. The top-heavy culture, with a few powerful directors in charge, was designed to keep order.

Flexibility and localized control—Dr. Garcia's vision—was the enemy of the old order. As Haydee observed, his ideas were "pretty advanced revolutionary thought."

Under Dr. Garcia's decentralization plan, patients would live in wards with fellow patients who came from their own counties and towns, and staff was assigned to specific wards so they could establish personal connections with their patients, and even with the local public. After all, as pharmaceutical drugs allowed more patients to move back into their own towns and neighborhoods, it was practical for social workers to have a familiarity with those specific geographic areas as well, because they could help re-integrate their clients into the social life of their towns and cities.

"So, for example, social workers would have people in the local community to relate to about a patient's needs," Gregorio explained. "But they wouldn't have to worry about relating to the whole state of Iowa."

The power was shifting too. In the old order, the director of nursing decided the schedule for the entire institution, and each day's assignment flowed from her office to the rest of the institution's staff and the professional corps.

Under Dr. Garcia's new plan, each ward was assigned its own team. This team was composed of nurses, social workers, psychologists, recreational therapists, psychiatrists, and other professionals as needed. This small, personalized staff reported to the team leader of the ward, and every person on the team had closer, more personal knowledge of the needs of each individual patient.

The new team approach also included a huge swath of workers who had been pretty much discounted before: the ward staff. These workers, ironically, were the closest to the patients on a daily basis. They made sure each person was awake, dressed, fed, and ready for the day. Although they oversaw the daily life of each patient, these staff people were minimally trained and poorly paid. Perhaps worst of all, they were seen—and they saw themselves—as little more than guards and rule enforcers.

The Clarinda Plan upgraded the training and the responsibilities of these workers.

"The ward staff had to be trained to actually step out and talk to the patient," Gregorio explained. "It wasn't only custodial anymore, and it wasn't about being 'boss' of the ward, it was about being really *invested* in the treatment, in how we treat the patients...they had to feel a commitment in what happens to the patient, that they had a role in the patient's welfare, and that their suggestions were taken seriously."

No surprise, the ward staff and team members were energized by their new responsibilities, which gave meaning and purpose to their interactions with patients. And no surprise, the hierarchy were livid to see themselves shorn of power.

And yet, despite the top-heavy grumblings, when the patients' individual needs began to be taken into account, other lights began to break through. For example, as much as Thorazine and other drugs represented an historic medical milestone in mental health, Gregorio and Haydee discovered through experience that these drugs, powerful as they were, didn't help every patient in the same way. Instead, each individual needed their own combinations of a certain specific drug along with psychotherapy, group support and individual care. And some patients didn't need drugs at all.

This realization, in turn, fueled the progress of psychotherapy, which recognized that recovery from mental illness doesn't always rest solely on medical and pharmaceutical help. Behavioral therapy can also heal. Gregrorio and Haydee saw this behavioral element immediately, and they responded by forming psycho-therapy groups and putting more emphasis on their own skills as psychotherapists.

In Dr. Garcia's new system, Haydee was assigned to be a team leader with some clinical responsibilities, and Gregorio was a psy-chiatrist assigned to specific wards. They were energized by their assignments, which were custom-designed to fit their personal skills and talents. For Haydee, her preference was administration, for Gregorio, it was clinical work.

There was one other thing: Dr. Garcia had the vision, but he left it up to Gregorio and Haydee to figure out how to implement it.

Something else had to be considered too. The directors of the institution were furious.

∾

Today, Haydee and Gregorio can smile at the furor that developed, but at the time the upheaval in the hospital was a crisis of the first order, and it eventually sealed the fate of both Dr. Garcia and the two Drs. Kort.

The crisis was all about the threat to power.

Gregorio explained how the old order was under siege: "Before they changed to the Clarinda Plan, the director of nursing was responsible for all the nurses in the hospital. So she had to have a central office with a secretary and lots of staff to manage all the nurses. Every day the nurses had to check in with the central nursing office to know where they were assigned for that day, rather than knowing they were part of a team…then there was the director of social workers, and the director of psychologists, and so on. They felt they were losing total power, too. These were the people who were manipulating the community."

Manipulating the community?

Indeed. The combined old guard, threatened and angry, put their collective heads together to figure out how to fight back, and sure enough, they found a vulnerable spot—the patients' own hometowns and neighborhoods.

The vulnerability they exploited was that the Clarinda Plan called for re-integrating the mentally ill into their hometowns whenever possible. Thanks to new techniques and therapies, that goal was entirely reasonable. Powerful drugs, combined with psychotherapy and individual treatment plans, allowed many people who had been felled by mental illness to return to their homes and live full and happy lives, surrounded by their families and friends.

But first they had to be given the chance, and the institutional hierarchy resisted that. Their entire livelihoods and careers were invested in the status quo, which meant keeping patients inside the institution.

With deliberate and steady purpose, the powers-that-be started a whisper campaign that raised an alarm in neighborhoods, towns and counties until an apprehensive citizenry could not help but hear it. As Gregorio and Haydee recall well, the message was simple and devastating: *"These foreign doctors"* (Dr. Garcia-Bunuel, and Drs. Gregorio and Haydee Kort) *"don't know what they are doing and they're releasing dangerous patients to the community and we better do something about stopping them..."*

As Haydee and Gregorio recalled, the fury soon settled on their boss: "They cornered in on Dr. Garcia and accused him, *'You're endangering the community with all the crazy people that you're releasing.'"*

A fair fight was one thing, but it was impossible to fight shadows and irrational fears. The pressure was on. After Dr. Garcia was beaten up for a while, the killing blow came in a soft, final punch: *"You are very talented, but you have to take your talent somewhere else."*

Within a year, Dr. Luis Garcia-Bunuel, visionary, innovator, and mentor to Gregorio and Haydee Kort, had been forced out of his job.

Now what would the Drs. Kort do? As Gregorio put it, "Our sense was, 'We don't want to stay here if they're going to fire our mentor!'"

~

In Tennessee, a crisis of culture had forced the young doctors to move on. Now, less than two years later, they faced a crisis of leadership that would force their next move. And once again, a totally unexpected path was about to open up before them.

Soon after Dr. Garcia was forced out of his job in Clarinda (only to begin a far better prospect in New York), the annual meeting of the American Psychiatric Association was convening some 450 miles away in Chicago.

Gregorio and Haydee always enjoyed attending the annual meetings of the APA, and now, with their careers up in the air, they were not about to miss the networking opportunities at this one. Another participant was a Dr. Meng, who was the assistant superintendent at the Clarinda Mental Health Institute.

Dr. Meng had been pretty beaten up himself by the public controversy that had forced out Dr. Garcia, but he had held on to his job, and he was generally in favor of the Clarinda Plan. What's more, he recognized the value of the two young physicians who were now very much associated with the innovative system.

During a break in the proceedings, Dr. Meng fell to chatting with Dr. Willis Bower, the superintendent of the Colorado State Hospital in Pueblo, Colorado.

"By then the Clarinda Plan was already well thought of nationally," Gregorio explained, "and Dr. Bower was looking for people with experience with the Clarinda Plan to come to Pueblo and implement it."

Dr. Meng had a tip for the Pueblo superintendent: "We have two Dr. Korts working for us at Clarinda, and if you ever decided to hire them, they would be a big asset to you. I'd recommend them."

Laughing, Haydee recalled, "We hadn't even put in applications, and we didn't even know these conversations were going on!"

Sometime after the meeting in Chicago ended, Dr. Bower telephoned the young couple in Clarinda and arranged for them to visit the hospital in Pueblo.

The invitation came at just the right time, Haydee said: "We knew our time was short in Clarinda, because everybody who was supportive of us was gone."

The Clarinda Plan, and the two Drs. Kort, were about to move west.

Haydee holds the award for Woman of the Year 1983-84 presented by the League Club Business and Professional Women's organization.

"I wanted to create a beautiful environment for patients." Gregorio Kort in 1986, standing in front of the award-winning, nationally recognized art gallery project he brought to the hospital wards. His innovative ideas for making CSH a humanizing experience for patients came to include sporting events, ski outings and camping trips.

Gregorio's many innovations to enhance the experience of patients at CSH was recognized with this award presented in 1984, in honor of his work as Director of Adult Psychiatric Services. "It was particularly touching that they took the time with this award, and I will forever treasure this," Gregorio said.

"There is no higher honor than to receive an award from the Department of Psychiatry at the University of Colorado School of Medicine." Gregorio and Haydee were especially proud of these twin awards, presented to each of them individually, for their innovative efforts to create a strong working relationship with the influential psychiatric and medical community at the University of Colorado.

"This award was unexpected but very much appreciated." Haydee Kort was close to retirement when she was surprised with this national award from the American Association of Psychiatric Administrators.

Cooperation between management and the employees' union at Colorado State Hospital accomplished great things during the Korts' tenure. Gregorio and Haydee were especially proud to receive this appreciation award from AFSCME Local 123 when they retired.

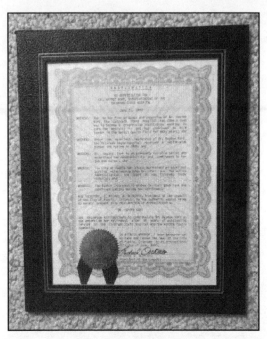

"Wow, I was proud of her!" Gregorio recalled the outpouring of affection for Haydee from the City of Pueblo, which issued this Proclamation shortly after the Korts retired in June 1990.

One of Haydee's and Gregorio's most cherished awards, given to them in 1990 by the staff and patients of the Colorado State Hospital at the time of their retirement.

CHAPTER SIX

"WE'LL MAKE HISTORY OR FALL ON OUR FACES"

At first sight, Pueblo, Colorado in the early 1960s wasn't easy to love.

"We took a train to Pueblo for our first interview, and no, our first impression of Pueblo wasn't very good," Haydee recalled, with a smile. The day-long train trip, from Clarinda to Pueblo, passed quickly through the lush cornfields of southeastern Iowa, straight west through the vast expanse of Kansas, before breaking onto the brown scrublands of southern Colorado.

As they approached Pueblo, if they squinted hard enough, Gregorio and Haydee might see the faint, graceful outlines of the Sangre de Cristo mountain range on the horizon. But up close, the sight was more grim. In the mid-twentieth century, Pueblo was a proud steel town that didn't hide its gritty manufacturing looks; it was a no-nonsense, hardworking blue-collar town of blast furnaces and fabrication mills. For train travelers lurching through the dismal railyards to the depot, even the huge doses of Colorado sunshine couldn't shake the impression of a town that was stern, gray, and utilitarian.

Gregorio and Haydee's destination, a forlorn Holiday Inn on

the poor side of town, didn't exactly brighten their spirits. And when they arrived for their job interview, their first impressions became more complicated.

The Colorado Insane Asylum, as it was first named, was founded in 1879, making it one of the first state hospitals to be established in the country. In that sense, it was ahead of its time, because it would take another decade before such state facilities were mandated by federal law.

The old photos show a stately but rather forbidding main building, sitting on a high hill, surrounded by a wide, scrubby lawn. Gregorio and Haydee knew they were not in lush, rain-drenched Iowa anymore! However, many years before the Korts arrived in 1961, the name had been changed to Colorado State Hospital, and by the time of their job interview there was a wide main drive and a boulevard of trees to soften the forbidding approach.

Gregorio and Haydee recalled well their first meeting with the newly appointed superintendent, the candid and direct Dr. Willis Bower. As Haydee remembered it, he wasted no time laying out the challenges they faced: "We had our first meeting with Dr. Bower in his office and he said, 'If you're going to judge the hospital by what you see here today, don't come.'"

It's easy to imagine the Korts' spirits slipping a few more notches. But the next thing the superintendent said illuminated his reputation as a leader of change: "But if you're going to come for what we're going to *do,* then you will be welcome."

So began a professional relationship that changed everything. Superintendent Willis Bower had built a prestigious reputation in Boston as a psychiatrist, a professor of psychiatry, and a psychotherapist. He left the elite environs of the east to run the Colorado

State Hospital thanks to no less than the personal endorsement of Colorado Governor Stephen McNichols, who handpicked Dr. Bower to fulfill his campaign promise to address the neglect of the state's mentally ill persons.

In fact, decades before the Korts arrived, overcrowding at the Colorado State Hospital was at a crisis pitch. No one ever got close to a permanent solution, because there were so many arguments and political pressures, and every proposal was met by controversy followed by stalemates and more fighting.

The lack of a permanent solution meant that even as early as 1923, patient enrollment was 2,400 and already growing out of control. That year, to relieve the pressure, a new building annex was purchased over the protests of the hospital superintendent himself, H.A. LaMoure.

The newly purchased, star-crossed facility was located an inconvenient two miles away from the main hospital and accessed only by crossing railroad tracks. And it wasn't long before Superintendent LaMoure's warnings about the property were vindicated in a tragic way: The building's hazardous location was confirmed when two patients and a nurse were struck and killed by a train, according to hospital history. Later, another building was acquired that was referred to far and wide as the White Elephant Annex. Its name alone showed how people felt about *that*. Meanwhile, patients kept coming. Photographs taken well into the 1950s document the unrelieved pressure, showing rows upon rows of patient beds stacked side by side and spilling out into the narrow hallways.

By 1961, the year Gregorio and Haydee arrived, the state mental hospital in Pueblo was responsible for six thousand patients, three times the size of the hospital in Clarinda, Iowa.

Bursting onto this chaotic scene, also in 1961, came Dr. Willis Bower, a tall, serious, and charismatic psychiatrist bristling with energy and determination. Recommended by the Colorado governor himself, Dr. Bower's sterling reputation was on the line. He had every incentive to break through the years of wrangling and finally implement a plan to relieve the inhumane overcrowding.

As he laid out his vision to his two young visitors from Iowa, he explained how he planned to adapt the Clarinda Plan to the needs of Colorado's much larger state hospital.

The working strategy in Colorado would have a similarly bulky name as it did in Iowa, "Pueblo State Hospital Geographic Decentralization." Bulky name, yes, but it described a modern, streamlined idea. Like the Iowa prototype, its core philosophy was to decentralize the state hospital system and provide more individualized care to each person with a mental illness. The ultimate goal would be to re-integrate each person back into their homes and communities.

From their first meeting, Gregorio and Haydee sensed they were in the presence of a leader who would make their professional lives worthwhile. "He had the best credentials possible," said Haydee, "and we were impressed by his sincerity."

Dr. Bower's commitment to upend the establishment was compelling. Almost sixty years later, the Korts share a laugh as they remember Dr. Bower's first promise to them:

"He said, 'I think we are going to do something significant here and make a big contribution to psychiatry, and if we don't, we'll all be looking for a job together!'"

Then, with quietly contained but unmistakable enthusiasm, Dr. Bower began to paint a portrait of his vision for the decentralization of the hospital system. Gregorio and Haydee would be staff psychiatrists working within a newly formed entity, a treatment facility, where each of them would be in charge of individually treating between 450 and 500 patients. The treatment plans would depend on the Korts' professional expertise; they would develop a medical treatment plan for each patient using the variety of therapies available in whatever combination they deemed appropriate. These individual treatments could include the new anti-psychotic drugs, psychotherapy, group therapy and yes, the controversial electroshock (which to this day is highly effective when used correctly).

In other words, patients at the Colorado State Hospital would be treated as individual human beings, with their own psychiatrist and medical team, just as if they were privately paying patients in the outside world. No longer would they be considered as nameless numbers, shoved into corners and abandoned day after day along shadowed hallways.

Yes, the patient load was daunting, but Dr. Bower wanted the Korts to know that they weren't expected to take on everything at once. "We are going to plan out what we do," Dr. Bower said, "so don't get concerned about how many patients you will be responsible for in the beginning." He explained there would be an orderly transition and implementation of the final plan. That was all ahead. For now, all the two Drs. Kort had to know was this: "This hospital is going to change completely and I'm going to see that it changes. If you want to be part of that, you can come."

Somehow Dr. Bower made even the difficulties seem like an adventure. With a firm handshake to each Dr. Kort, he concluded their first interview with another self-confident promise:

"Either we make history, or we fall flat on our faces."

~

Dr. Bower's cautionary warning, that the Korts should not to come to Pueblo based on what they would see that day, was not a throwaway comment. He wasn't looking for establishment puppets to enforce the status quo; he was looking for fellow revolutionaries who were suited up and ready for a challenge!

That's why he wanted Gregorio and Haydee to be prepared for what they saw that day. In fact, the Korts remember their first tour of the Colorado State Hospital in 1961 as shocking and sad.

"I'll never forget," Haydee said. "We walked on one of the patient wards, and the hallway had broken chairs lined all against the wall, and they were filled with patients all rocking on the chairs, up against the wall, totally out of it. They were neglected, just completely neglected.

"As we walked around, the main emotion we felt was sadness. And we thought, 'Oh my God, there's a lot to do here! There's a lot to be thinking about—what can we do?' To see all these people totally left to themselves with nothing to look forward to, and nobody to take care of them, except for ward attendants to feed them. Besides that, nothing was going on…and of course we had to take the word of Dr. Bower that there was going to be a treatment facility, and we would become part of that treatment facility, and it was our job to get those patients out of the shadows and the corners and into treatment so that we could work with them."

Surely the staff felt the same? Gregorio and Haydee had an appointment to meet the director of nursing, whom they assumed would soon become a trusted colleague, as eager as they were to improve the disturbing hospital conditions and implement Dr. Bower's vision.

Instead, to their shock, the director of nursing was barely civil to the young visiting psychiatrists. In a coldly businesslike way she snapped: "What do you mean, you intend to change everything? We have no intention of changing this place. If you came here to change anything, you might as well go back."

Her reaction was as troubling and eye-opening as the state of the teeming and demoralized wards. "It was fantastic," said Haydee, "fantastically sad."

That night, Gregorio and Haydee went back to their shabby little hotel room and looked at each other. Yes, they had each been offered a job to help build an entirely new and humane system for mental health treatment. But the entrenched establishment was not going down without a fight. The rude reaction from the director of nursing proved that. This would not be an easy decision. Clearly, they were facing serious opposition, even outright hostility. But they had to make a choice.

"Beba, shall we do it, or should we look at other places?" Goyo said. "Of course there are other options we can try, other places to look, or (this he said half-jokingly) we can even go back to Argentina!"

He saw something in his young wife's eyes, and knew her answer. Goyo and Beba were together on this one: "*Yes, let's take this opportunity and see what we can do.*"

Six decades later, they reflected on the decision that changed their lives.

"Somehow, we were infected with the optimism of Dr. Bower, and we felt this could be done," Gregorio said.

Added Haydee, "We knew he wasn't lying to us, and that he was going to do great things which we could be a part of. We believed he really meant it. We *had* to believe him, or forget it."

∼

Of course, life doesn't run along in straight lines, or on only one narrow path. As Gregorio and Haydee weighed their decision to come to Pueblo, Colorado, they also had to think about their young family, about uprooting their infant son Marcelo from Iowa, and what their family would be thinking back home in Argentina.

After all, they had only been in the country for four years, and already they had moved to more states in the USA than many native Americans! Their swift progress from Tennessee to Iowa to Colorado was remarkable, but it also painted a picture of their future which could not be ignored. Although it would be another few years before they became American citizens (in 1963), it was already clear that Gregorio and Haydee were not coming back to Argentina. For their parents, that prospect brought heartbreak mixed with a fierce pride at what their children had accomplished.

Wrapping up things in Iowa was easier. Their champion, Dr. Luis Garcia-Bunuel, had been driven away by the Clarinda establishment, and with him went any hope the Korts had of a meaningful future in Iowa. If they had any lingering doubt of that, it was driven away by the grudging and ungracious farewell of Dr. Garcia's successor when they turned in their resignations: "Well, we thought you were only temporary employees anyway."

His cold indifference served only to lighten their hearts—yes, leaving Clarinda was the right thing to do. Personal goodbyes were harder. Little Marcelo had been cared for by an older woman, a wonderfully loyal and competent nanny, who said when they left: "You are taking my life away!" Leaving her was as painful as leaving the unforgettable Vaserine in Bolivar.

Still, it was impossible not to be excited about the future, which began the morning the Kort family set off in their '53 Oldsmobile for Colorado. Their slender list of belongings followed in a moving van. They rented a two-bedroom basement apartment in a house at 47 Caledonia Street, located in a sweet residential neighborhood called Belmont, and began to make friends.

The hospital wasn't close, but it wasn't far away either. As Gregorio put it with a laugh, "Nothing is far away in Pueblo."

~

It wasn't long before Gregorio and Haydee discovered that they faced two enemies. One was hostility, which the director of nursing had revealed with all the subtlety of a boxer's left hook.

The other enemy was equally fierce, but deceptively wrapped in a velvet glove. Its name was indifference.

Indifference—the refusal to recognize or relieve the suffering of others—was revealed in soothing stages by an assistant administrator. Over time, he made it clear that the needs of the patients were less important than maintaining the power structure of the status quo. He communicated this politely during meetings with a dismissive half smile, a shrug of the shoulders, a change of subject. But it didn't take long for the Korts to piece together his message:

"Nothing is gonna change because I'm here, and Dr. Bower is an outsider, and he doesn't know what he's talking about."

Gregorio and Haydee were young, inspired, and challenge-ready. They knew that the status quo and its stubborn and inflexible way of thinking was long past its prime. So whatever resistance was ahead—from the nursing director, the other administrators, and the rest of the establishment at the Colorado State Hospital—surely would not last.

Said Haydee, "We didn't believe it would, because we thought these people couldn't actually have any more power than Dr. Bower. All they could do was talk."

CHAPTER SEVEN

THE POWERS THAT BE

"We thought these people couldn't actually have any more power than Dr. Bower. All they could do was talk."

Confident and determined as Haydee was when she expressed that idea in 1961, when she and Gregorio joined the Pueblo State Hospital they quickly learned that Dr. Bower had poked a monster-sized hornet's nest. The hospital hierarchy had no intention of surrendering its cozy hive of power. They fought and stung with everything they had to prevent Dr. Bower and his two newest innovators from knocking down their entrenched system.

Until Dr. Bower arrived on the scene in 1961, the power had been concentrated among a few people in charge. Now the new superintendent, drawing from the groundbreaking Clarinda Plan, was implementing the geographic decentralization concept in Colorado. The new system would create teams, each team headed by a psychiatrist, that would operate in six newly created statewide divisions. This localized concept allowed the system to become flexible and responsive to the needs of each patient.

As Dr. Bower's newly hired staff psychiatrists, Dr. Gregorio Kort and Dr. Haydee Kort were to be key leaders of the new team concept, which was composed of nurses, social workers, psychologists, recreational therapists, psychiatric technicians, and other support staff.

Even though Gregorio and Haydee were just two among a larger group of psychiatrists, it was clear Dr. Bower saw them as having a greater role as teachers and motivators. As early participants in the original masterwork, the Clarinda Plan, the two young psychiatrists from Argentina had an understanding of the concept of localized care that was invaluable in reorganizing the entire system. In no small way, they could help translate the plan to the rest of the teams.

Gregorio and Haydee were put in charge of between 450 and 500 patients each. Gregorio was in charge of the Southeast Division, comprising the huge swath of southern Colorado. His responsibility was to lead the Southeast Division teams and work directly with the patients, which was the career emphasis he hoped for when he first began to practice psychiatry.

Haydee's role was to run the Colorado Springs Division. Together, the Korts faced an antiquated system roiling in chaos. Over the years, it had devolved into an "open door policy" where virtually any suffering soul who walked through the door gained admittance. By the mid-twentieth century, the hospital had solidified its image as a magnet for any behavior outside the norm.

In fact, long before the two Drs. Kort arrived in Pueblo, the hospital's address had become both a semi-humorous threat and a punchline to a joke: "You better behave," went the saying, "or you'll get sent to 13th Street!"

The barbs reflected a true weakness of the system: the standards of admission were low enough to admit almost anyone, from the seriously disturbed individual to the volatile family nuisance.

Nor was there much effort expended to differentiate between people who had true psychiatric illnesses and those who had behavior and emotional problems, or who were mentally debilitated simply because of advanced age.

Under Dr. Bower's newly developing system, the only people who qualified for entry were the truly mentally ill. Other groups that needed care (such as the elderly, and people with highly treatable emotional and behavior issues) were placed in appropriate nursing homes, or given access, as needed, to medication and outside counseling services.

The result was the breaking up of a system that had become little more than a warehouse for human beings. Eventually, under this streamlined plan, the Colorado State Hospital at Pueblo was able to reduce its intake from six thousand patients to just six hundred, while still providing higher levels of care to those who remained, as well as to those who were treated and able to return to their communities.

The plan turned out to be so effective and successful, Gregorio said, that mental health institutions from around the country were making the trek to Pueblo, Colorado to see how it was done.

Of course, these massive changes threatened the existence of the status quo. That's why, when Dr. Bower first explained his vision to the Korts, he added a warning: "Whatever we're going to do, it's not going to work with the director of nursing or the assistant superintendent. Those two are going to be against us."

∾

It didn't take long for the pushback to begin. Shortly after Dr. Bower's arrival, Haydee said, the opposition began skirmishing to regain control:

"I had 450 patients and worked from 7:30 in the morning to maybe 7:00 at night," Haydee said. "The ward staff was eager to see changes on the wards, and I'm working with each patient and accomplishing something. Then one day I come in, and ten of my patients are gone."

Incredulous, Haydee asked her staff: "What happened to them?"

The boldest person on the ward staff stepped forward to explain: "The director of nursing sent them to the dairy farm."

The dairy farm was one of the many areas on the sprawling hospital grounds that used patient labor. Other patients were assigned to the laundry, the kitchen, the cleaning staff, and a myriad of other departments. This antiquated assignment system was a major part of what Dr. Bower and the Drs. Kort planned to abolish.

It was not that they didn't see *work* as having therapeutic value. Far from it! The problem was that patients were being lumped into wards according to their work *categories,* rather than being allowed to live and interact with fellow patients who shared similar backgrounds and local culture. The geographic decentralization plan was predicated on the idea that more patients could be healed if they were treated as valued individuals who had hometowns, family histories and, perhaps most important, communities where they could someday return to live again.

As Gregorio and Haydee eased into their new jobs, they were hearing more and more stories about how, under the old structure, care of patients was at best indifferent, and at the worst, downright inhumane.

The Korts recalled one especially sad case involving a patient, and a guard who thrived on intimidation. For years, the guard had put this patient on "extra duty." Besides his regular daily tasks, the patient was ordered to wash the guard's personal car every week. Under the corrupted system the hapless patient had been reduced to a life of servitude, forced to perform personal favors for someone with power over him.

Then the Korts learned of another disturbing incident which had been churning in the rumor mill before they arrived:

One day, as one of the administrators was passing by, a patient leaped from her chair and attacked him. The shaken-up pooh-bah immediately ordered that the patient be sent to a secluded room and put in physical restraints. After the door slammed shut, the overworked staff turned their attention back to their endless "to do" list, and the patient was forgotten. Thankfully, an alert employee rescued the scuffler before she came to serious harm, but the incident further confirmed that the powers-that-be saw the patients not as individuals, but as numbers. Clearly, the hierarchy had no compassion or insight into their residents. Haydee put it bluntly: "They were bad people."

Without brakes, the trend was unmistakable. Colorado State Hospital was morphing into a prison for indentured servants rather than a skilled institution dedicated to help suffering human beings who needed clinical evaluation and individual therapies. Worst of all, no one was in place to advocate for patients, or to motivate them to get better.

So, on the day Haydee found out the director of nursing had surreptitiously ordered patients to work at the dairy farm—well, that was like shaking a red flag in front of a champion bull! Sixty years later, Haydee's reaction is as fiery and vivid as the day it happened: "I said, "Well, the director of nursing is a very strong person, but so am I."

Haydee immediately snatched up the phone and called the head nurse. "I said, 'I'm Dr. Kort and I'm in charge of these patients and as long as I'm in charge of these patients, you don't move anyone ever again.'"

"Who do you think you are?" the nursing director barked. "You don't know what you're talking about!"

"Okay, let's go to Dr. Bower's office and find out what he would approve of," Haydee shot back. "We'll find out whether you can move the patients to the farm, or whether you must leave the patients where they are, so I can treat them."

Haydee chuckled at the memory. "So I ran to the office, and she almost beat me to it. When we got there, Dr. Bower told the nursing director, 'You have no business moving patients unless Dr. Kort agrees to it. There will be no more moving of patients without her approval, or the approval of whichever physician happens to be on duty.'"

Long after the confrontation in the superintendent's office, the director of nursing was still fuming. Haydee tried to reason with her. "I'm just a doctor here working for Dr. Bower, and trying to do what Dr. Bower thinks is right, and what I think needs to be done," she recalled saying. The head nurse's response, in so many words, was clear: *"Okay, perhaps Dr. Bower agrees with you, but we have the power, so let's see how far you get."*

The Korts soon discovered the true roles of the director of nursing and one of the other administrators. "They ran the hospital," Haydee said. "Every patient had to be checked in by them, and they moved them around wherever they wanted to, wherever they needed work done. It was incredible what was going on."

Haydee knew she couldn't be pushed around because she had Dr. Bower on her side. What's more, her own character and determination wouldn't allow it.

Still, it soon became clear that the fight wasn't over, and the powers-that-be simply shifted strategies. Maybe they could make the Korts *themselves* miserable? Sure enough, it wasn't long before the Korts were called into an administrator's office and ordered to report for duty on Saturday mornings. That order not only would lengthen their work week to five and a half days, but would deprive them of cherished home time with their small son.

"No, I'm not going to work five and a half days, because Dr. Bower hired us to work Monday through Friday, *not* on Saturday mornings," Haydee said. "And if you don't agree with that, you go and ask Dr. Bower."

Today, Haydee and Gregorio can laugh at the incident and its aftermath: "No, we did *not* have to work Saturday mornings!"

After that, the opposition began to back off, at least in obvious ways, "the kind of ways where they could throw their weight around," as Haydee put it. In fact, in due time, the outcome plotted for Dr. Bower and the two Drs. Kort was blown back on their opponents. Within six months of the arrival of Dr. Bower and the Korts, the hospital's "old guard," including the director of nursing, announced their retirements.

It looked like Dr. Bower and his innovators had knocked down the hive. Or so it seemed.

With the old guard seemingly swept away and a new, motivated staff assembled, Gregorio and Haydee finally had the freedom they needed to complete the patient care revolution that had begun in Clarinda, Iowa and had been adapted by Dr. Willis Bower to the Colorado State Hospital.

Clearly, Dr. Bower was aware of the power of continuity. In the first six months of his tenure (which coincided with the arrival of Gregorio and Haydee), the new superintendent made a bold move. He reached out to a figure from Gregorio and Haydee's past, and hired their old boss from Iowa, Dr. Luis Garcia-Bunuel.

In one perceptive hiring decision, Dr. Bower showed he was determined to follow through on the Clarinda promise. Who better to implement the innovations that began there than the innovator himself?

Dr. Garcia, as he was known, joined Colorado State Hospital as Clinical Director, one of the most influential positions in the hospital system. In that role, he would be working closely with the Korts (and all the teams of psychiatrists and their support staffs) to create a system that would put the patients first.

For Gregorio and Haydee, their old boss was a welcome sight indeed. Not only did they share Spanish, the language of their birth, but in Iowa, their two families had already formed a natural friendship. Dr. Garcia and his wife had a child about the same age as Marcelo, and they enjoyed getting together for evening dinners of Spanish paella and tangy gazpacho while the kids romped happily in the back yard. The Korts and the Garcia-Bunuels also shared a deepening love for their adopted country, the USA, and a love for their profession of psychiatry, which was now being put to the test in a hospital that desperately needed their expertise.

Intense and fiery, Dr. Garcia was not a retiring personality anchored to his desk. His driving presence and rapid-fire speech, redolent of his Spanish roots, quickly caught the attention of not only the hospital but also the Pueblo community.

Did his foreign background make people uneasy? Perhaps. Unlike Gregorio and Haydee, who say they were always welcomed in Pueblo and never sensed any discrimination, the same may not have been true of Dr. Garcia. Did his ties to famous film-director uncle, Luis Bunuel, who was known for his avant-garde films, gin up the Pueblo rumor mill and create suspicion?

In any case, anxieties about Dr. Garcia would fester in the wider Pueblo community, and eventually break into the open. But not yet.

As for Dr. Bower, he was an equally forceful personality, very different in temperament and background from Dr. Garcia but just as charismatic, and undeniably his own man. Even today, the Korts smile fondly at the memory of the difficult, magnetic, and Boston-bred Dr. Bower. Many of the staff were frightened by his steely manner, but not the Korts, who remember him with deep affection.

"We 'got' him," as Haydee said. "We appreciated his manner. Yes, he was rigid, and people were afraid of him, but we understood him. He had hired us and because of that I think we were rather special to him."

Nevertheless, like everyone else, Gregorio and Haydee remember how discomfiting Dr. Bower's presence could be. When he walked into a meeting, everyone in the room immediately switched to high alert. Aloof and always impeccably dressed, the superintendent radiated supreme self-control and command of the room.

His self-assured demeanor never gave anything away. He never betrayed a hint of temper, nor was he given to effusive praise.

"He never answered anything in anger," Gregorio said. Instead, when confronted by staff complaints, he listened intently for a while, then told the speaker in his polite and controlled way exactly why he or she would not win that argument. "His manner was, 'Well, believe me, I understand how you feel, but let me clarify what the reality is…'"

His cool persona meant the staff looked forward to Dr. Bower's regularly scheduled meetings with the enthusiasm of someone facing open-heart surgery.

"Everybody feared going to those meetings because he was so tough," Haydee recalled.

Dr. Bower would listen to staff reports, but for only so long. He hated drawn-out meetings, and wasting time was anathema. At those meetings, Haydee said, "He expected the people reporting to him to be intelligent when they spoke, and not say stupid things. He would say to somebody, 'Why are you bringing that up in this meeting? It has nothing to do with what we're talking about.' And that didn't play out well."

Haydee added, "Gregorio and I appreciated him because we could recognize that he could differentiate between the good things that had to be accomplished, and the irrelevant things that needed to be thrown away."

Another quality of Dr. Bower's style was his resistance to giving praise. That meant that people would hold their breaths at his meetings, hoping *not* to be singled out, because to be ignored probably meant their work was acceptable. But if Dr. Bower's eyes raked over the crowd, fastened on you, and then called out your name? Well, it didn't mean that you were getting a medal; no, any attention at all meant that you had probably done something wrong.

No doubt about it, Dr. Bower was a man who produced results at the hospital, but did not necessarily inspire an emotional love from his staff.

Years later, long after Dr. Bower had moved on and Haydee had taken his job as superintendent, the two happened to see each other at a medical conference in Arizona. To this day, Haydee recalls the exchange because of the glimpse it offered into a man whose leadership skills had always exuded control and cool restraint. Now she saw other undercurrents in his personality, including a touching and likeable self-understanding.

"At the time, I was already superintendent," Haydee recalled. "Dr. Bower said to me, 'Haydee, how do you get people to do what you want them to do?'"

And I said, "Dr. Bower, my goodness, I mean it's such a basic question, I guess I don't know exactly how to answer..."

Her old boss was looking at her intently, and was clearly so sincere about the question that she continued. "It's a matter of working with people, you have to take the time to understand their point of view, and you praise them, and then you explain where you are coming from, and you hope to win them over..."

To put it simply, Haydee concluded, "It's a matter of winning their support."

The former superintendent listened thoughtfully and then said, "Well, I could never get that."

Haydee never forgot his startling and honest admission. The reserved and self-confident former leader, considered fearsome by so many, had shown a vulnerability that only increased her already great respect for him.

~

During his tenure, the complicated Dr. Bower, austere in manner but highly respected, continued to produce results. He had withstood pushback from the old guard, who finally surrendered or retired. With formal opposition apparently ended, Dr. Bower and his teams, with Gregorio and Haydee taking leadership roles among the psychiatrists, began to change the entire system of the Colorado State Hospital.

Since its founding as the Colorado Insane Asylum in 1879, the hospital wards, where the patients lived and slept, were built to be safe and clean, but conceptually they were akin to cellblocks where unruly people were meant to be kept in line by employees who were at best performing what amounted to guard duties.

All that changed under the Dr. Bower regime. The role of staff who worked on a daily basis with patients was reevaluated. Those staff who showed an empathy with patients and an affinity for taking on new skills were retrained to take on greater responsibilities. As a reflection of the seriousness of their roles, they were given a new name, *psychiatric technicians.* In their new capacity, they were taught how to interact with patients and how to evaluate their needs, and their daily, one-on-one experiences with individual patients gave the psychiatric team valuable insights into planning appropriate treatments.

A new category, a janitorial staff, was created to maintain the basic cleaning and orderliness that had been previously expected of the "guards."

With a strong support staff as its foundation, the way was open to provide true mental health care, starting with Gregorio and Haydee and each of the psychiatrists in charge. "We were providing leadership to the social workers, psychologists, and psychiatric technicians to provide actual treatment, rather than just custodial care," Haydee said.

At the core of their success were the newly trained psychiatric technicians, who were taught the skills to work with individual patients on a daily basis.

"Their input to us was invaluable," Gregorio said. "Of course, we couldn't have a complete knowledge of each individual patient's history, but now the staff was filling us in, and slowly but surely we were getting it. The other thing that made the psychiatric technicians so important was the fact that they had a daily relationship with the patients, and they could help the patients understand, 'This is not the end of the road; we are going to give you the correct medications and treatments that will help you achieve the goal of getting you back to your community and your family.'"

However, a basic question was, who needed continued hospitalization and who could benefit from returning to their communities and hometowns?

"There were many of those patients who really didn't need to be in a hospital," Haydee said. "Many of them had just been dumped there. By working with the staff, we narrowed down the number of patients that we were working with and that needed treatment, as opposed to the ones that had been dumped there, and could benefit from other kinds of help. The staff helped us sort it all out."

There was one more critical and fundamental change in patient categories: Until then, people with developmental disabilities had been lumped into wards along with the mentally ill, even though these were two profoundly distinct and separate categories of need. Yet tragically, in the many years of the hospital's existence (and in common with standard mental health care at the time), people with developmental disabilities—that is, with cognitive defects such as severe learning and communication disabilities brought on by brain trauma—were swept into the same categories and living situations as the mentally ill, who suffered from psychiatric behavioral disorders such as schizophrenia, depression and anxiety.

In Dr. Bower's era, these two acutely different kinds of human suffering were finally recognized as needing separate care, and in separate places.

In what had become no less than another revolution in mental health care, Dr. Bower had proven to be a true leader, and he had confirmed the trust Gregorio and Haydee had decided to put in him when they took on the Pueblo challenge. "We thought at the time, there cannot be a better superintendent, or a better leader to effect all these changes," Gregorio recalled, "or anyone better to address the problems that may come from the community. He's the one."

But much remained to be done, and challenges loomed. For one thing, how do you reconfigure the living arrangements of an entire hospital system? And how do you physically move the six thousand patients who live there?

Again, Dr. Bower showed his astonishing command of the situation. He called in the United States Army.

CHAPTER EIGHT

MAKING PSYCHIATRIC HISTORY

On the morning of March 2, 1962, a long phalanx of U.S. Army personnel in trucks, jeeps and buses rumbled through the streets of Pueblo toward the state hospital. As military maneuvers go, this was no ordinary boots-on-the-ground campaign. The marching orders called for the Army to transport thousands of psychiatric patients from their old hospital wards to wards which reflected the new geographic designations of the decentralized plan.

This friendly "invasion" of Army troops, proposed by Dr. Bower and supported by Governor Stephen McNichols, was accomplished over two days. It represented the visionary concept of geographic decentralization finally brought to life.

Standing alongside Dr. Bower and Dr. Garcia at this historic crossroads, Gregorio and Haydee Kort watched the troop movements with a sense of accomplishment and professional pride. Barely into their early thirties and just five years in America, the young couple were at the center of the most enlightened revolution in mental health care since the arrival of anti-psychotic drugs in the mid-1950s.

Not only were the Korts at the center of this latest revolution, from the beginning, they were actively involved in making it happen.

"We already had the philosophy that we came with from the Clarinda Plan in Iowa," Haydee said. "We knew that many of those patients really didn't need to be in a hospital, they just had been dumped there. Now we were providing leadership to social workers, psychologists, nurses and psychiatric technicians to provide the correct individualized treatment for each patient, rather than generic custodial care."

Across the country, equally overburdened mental hospitals were watching the Pueblo movement with great interest. Few institutions had as many as the six thousand patients living at the Colorado State Hospital. Yet it had become clear that the nineteenth-century solution to help the mentally ill with basic custodial care was not only outdated, it had led to a dangerously overcrowded system that had become unresponsive to patients' welfare.

Now, in Colorado, a leadership team had figured out how to safely release the pressure cap and implement modern methods that would truly help the mentally ill. "There was incredible interest in all the state hospitals in the country, that decentralization was the way to deal with the accumulation of thousands of patients," Gregorio said.

So when the Clarinda Plan was adapted to Colorado's crisis and the Army was brought in to make things happen, there was no question about it: "This was a national event."

The carefully planned, organized commotion gripped everyone's attention, from administrators and politicians, to reporters and the citizens of Pueblo. In the flurry and disruption of the moment, one group of participants was quieter than the rest, even though their lives would change the most.

"The general reaction among the patients was, they were elated,"

Haydee said. "After many, many years living their lives assigned to one ward, finally they were getting out. Yes, they were excited. The overall mood was, 'Finally, we're going to get help.'"

For two days, Gregorio and Haydee and the hospital team worked alongside the military personnel. "We helped with patients to assure that they didn't get into any difficulty," Haydee said.

Methodically, with respect and gentleness, Army personnel helped patients into military buses, each bus bound for one of the six designated divisions. Of course, the severely mentally ill would remain at the hospital. About half the population (three thousand people) was composed of geriatric patients, and most of them remained at the hospital too, which was the only home many of them had ever known. The elderly patients who could, moved back with family or into nursing homes.

For the rest, the world was opening up to them again. Buses transported the patients to the division that corresponded with their own towns and neighborhoods. Some would live in a smaller group home or an outpatient setting, others would be reunited with their own families. Supervisory oversight still existed but it was localized. Professional teams composed of psychiatrists, psychologists, nurses, psychiatric technicians and support personnel were assigned to each division, and they were now responsible for following up on the welfare of the patients in their newly customized settings.

The task was daunting. In two days, the Fort Carson maneuver relocated six thousand patients, living in 250 wards, spread throughout several buildings, on large hospital grounds. This had never been done before. No one knew if it would work smoothly, or what unexpected problems would surface.

In fact, the glitches and hitches, anticipated and braced for, never happened. Yes, there was concern for certain patients who, in the run-up to the two-day event, had become agitated and shown signs of illness. The Army came medically prepared for every health crisis. But once the maneuvers were underway, stress seemed to vanish. "No patients became upset," Haydee marveled. "You never know how they're going to react, but it was amazing. They went along with the maneuvers just like you and I would."

There was only one incident: a doctor fell and broke his leg. "But there wasn't a single injury to patients," Haydee said.

The maneuvers proved to be a win-win for everyone, for the patients, the military, the hospital administration, right up to the governor himself.

"Fort Carson took it as training maneuvers, and they were very happy to have that opportunity," Gregorio said. "The governor was very happy because part of his direction was, 'Well, now that we are getting this underway, please remember that I promised people to do something for the mentally ill, so whatever you do, this has to be in the papers because it is very important PR!'"

Needless to say, public relations *were* important, and the governor wasn't the only one bracing for blowback. While the physical relocation was accomplished with military precision, across Colorado the news that thousands of mental patients were being released into their communities and hometowns had produced a level of anxiety, upset, and resistance that still had to be addressed.

That was certainly true in Pueblo, a "company town" when it came to the venerable old hospital on 13th Street. A new superintendent had roared in and forced out the longtime, high-level staff, including the nursing director and assistant administrators.

These displaced leaders, highly respected in the community, were somebody's neighbors, family, and friends. Rumors ran thick; did they retire, or were they fired? And mentally ill patients were being released back into neighborhoods and towns! What was going on?

In fact, long before the Fort Carson maneuvers, Gregorio and Haydee, along with the rest of the hospital team, were aware of a low, muttering buzz of discontent in Pueblo, and it wasn't hard to figure out the source.

"Some of the top-level people at the state hospital were agitating the community because they were losing power," Gregorio said.

Haydee added, "Then there was the threat that these new programs were going to get the patients out of the hospital's control and back into their own communities, and who knows what they're going to do there? It was okay as long as they were locked up."

To address the unrest, in the summer of 1961, nine months before the Fort Carson maneuvers, Dr. Bower had called together his staff, which he rebuilt with his own people. He told his team that he planned to alert the public ahead of time to the massive relocation effort. Everything must be handled with openness and transparency.

"He wanted to draw in the community and bring them on board to explain what would happen," Gregorio said. "All of us on Dr. Bower's leadership team agreed. 'Okay, we are going to do it,' we said, 'but let's set a date when it will happen so everybody will know ahead of time. That way there will be no attacks on the plan by anybody.'"

Everyone, from the governor to the news media to the public, was alerted, and March 1 and 2, 1962 were circled in red on Colorado's collective calendar. So far, so good. Then the history-making moment arrived and the two-day maneuvers went off without a hitch.

Did that mark the end to a troubling period of change and challenge?

Actually, the challenges had just begun.

~

Still, basking in the goodwill of the moment, the Pueblo Geographic Decentralization Plan developed by Dr. Bower and Dr. Garcia was a triumph in ways both large and small. The governor had the "important PR" he needed, and the two doctors, along with Dr. Gregorio Kort and Dr. Haydee Kort, had seen the culmination of years of vision and planning.

A new stability emerged, with Gregorio in charge of the Southeast Division, including the San Luis Valley, and with Haydee heading the Colorado Springs Division. Later on, she also was named Assistant Clinical Director and assigned to work alongside Dr. Garcia.

Behind the scenes, there were quieter triumphs that were even more touching because they were so unexpected. From behind the grim grey walls of an old hospital, individuals were emerging who were learning how to live again.

Ned was one of them. "Ned had been in the hospital for forty years," Gregorio recalled. "He was a paranoid schizophrenic, but he was no danger to anyone; he never assaulted or disturbed another person…"

Ned's problem was that he felt other people were trying to poison him. Gregorio recalled his long-ago patient with affection. "He had to drink from a certain container, because the water in any other container would be poison. It was the same with food. We would talk with him and say, 'Why don't you want to take that food, that water?' 'Because it's poison,' he would say. 'But you do see all the other patients, they are able to eat and drink from every plate and every glass, and nothing happens to them!'"

With great reasonableness, Ned would look at Gregorio and the other staff and reply calmly, "Yes, isn't it amazing what they can do just to me?"

In preparation for the decentralization move, "We finally managed to contact Ned's family," Gregorio said. "It consisted of two elderly sisters. We persuaded them to come and visit their brother at the hospital, and they did.

"The visit turned out to be very nice," Gregorio continued. "So the sisters said to us, 'His manners are very good. He's not acting disturbed, or threatening anyone. Can we take him home for a visit?'

"And of course," Gregorio said, with a smile, "they never brought him back."

Then there was the patient Haydee calls "Mary." She was a talented businesswoman from Denver whose productive life had been shattered by depression.

"She was a very good individual," Haydee recalled, "educated and bright, but she was extremely depressed, so much so that she couldn't function. She said, 'I can't take this life anymore, I can't live this way.'

"We had tried antidepressants but they didn't quite do the job," Haydee recalled. "She did not come out of her depression."

Haydee suspected she might have a solution for Mary, that she would benefit from electroshock treatments. To this day, electroshock remains a valuable psychiatric tool when used correctly, with the right patient. Haydee had used it at Iowa State Hospital with excellent results. Haydee ran a battery of tests to determine whether Mary was a candidate. She was, and three electroshock treatments followed. Normally, more than three treatments are needed, but in Mary's case, three was just right, and the result was astonishing: "She became a new person, the person that she was before she became depressed," Haydee said.

Of course, electroshock is not a be-all and end-all; only in the public's mind is it a matter of "zap and all is well." It is a serious option for the severely depressed patient, done in a surgical setting, and meant to be used in conjunction with other therapies, such as antidepressants. So it was with Mary. But what was astonishing in her case was the complete transformation of her life: she was able to move back to her hometown of Denver, opened a new retail shop downtown, and became a successful businesswoman once again. Her life was restored.

"Mary was on a suicidal path," Haydee said, "and in her case, electroshock was a lifesaver."

That's not to say there weren't heartbreaking cases. Some families refused to welcome their relative home, even though they were assured he or she was not dangerous. But others stepped forward and filled the gap. These were the boarding-home operators who were trained by the hospital's psychiatric teams to run a safe and welcoming new style of home for qualified patients.

"We trained the boarding-home owners to work with the patient," Haydee said. "So if the family wouldn't take him back, we would place him in a boarding home and maintain a relationship with that boarding-home operator. Patients functioned pretty well there. Actually, it was amazing how well they did, living with other patients."

Some psychiatric technicians opted to open boarding homes themselves, and that added a valuable level of expertise and oversight. In fact, the expansion of the responsibilities and roles of the psychiatric technicians was one of Gregorio and Haydee's major contributions to the new era. The role was refined and separated from the old-school idea of a "guard" (whose duties careened from keeping patients in line to sweeping the floors), into a serious position that required extra training in patient care and evaluation.

Sometimes, startling levels of cooperation sprang up out of nowhere. One of those occurred in Boone, a small town just twenty-five miles due east of Pueblo. As the head of the Pueblo Division, Gregorio saw the story unfold beginning to end:

"An elderly lady bought an old hotel in Boone that she wanted to revive," he recalled. "We saw an opportunity there, and we got busy talking to her. Rather than reviving the hotel, we asked if she would be interested in turning her hotel into a boarding home for eighteen patients that were about to be released, but they need some oversight and care. Would she be interested in that? She agreed!"

To prepare the patients for their new home, the psychiatric technician assigned to the patients' group therapy session was able to introduce the topic of the move in a measured and gentle way. And on the assigned day, those eighteen patients, mentally prepped for the big change, moved to their new boarding home. The psychiatric technician continued to meet them there for group therapy.

It many unexpected ways, the innkeeper turned boarding home

owner in Boone turned out to be a resourceful asset. She instinctively understood the spirit of this new mental health revolution, and she plunged in to make it work.

"We expected, and rightly so, that there would be a lot of concern with people saying, 'Who are these eighteen "crazy" patients?'" Gregorio said. "'How will they be integrated into our community?' Well, the boarding-home owner was very clever and very good. She got the patients all cleaned up, especially on Sundays, and began to take them to a church in the community."

Gregorio continued, "Of course some of the church members were upset that *these people* were coming to their church." With a laugh, he added, "Then, slowly but surely, the congregation realized that there were worse people coming to the church than these mentally ill people, so finally they accepted them!"

A quiet but profound way of thinking began to take root. Until then, society's prevailing view was that people with disabilities, including mental illness, were destined to remain stuck on the receiving end of other people's good works and charity.

Now, a startling new thought was emerging: "Why can't people with disabilities be *givers* of good works?" The eighteen men in the boarding home began taking on projects. First, they cleaned up a park. "That created a big shot of self-appreciation among them," Gregorio said.

With familiarity, barriers fell: "Then, people in the community started to stop by to pick them up to go to church, or to church picnics. The lady who ran the boarding home began working with the psychiatric technician, and together they came up with new projects that the patients could take into the community."

The collaboration was new, unexpected, and worked

spectacularly well. Keenly sensitive to the factors that encourage and motivate both staff and patients, Gregorio persuaded the psychiatric technician involved with the boarding home to write a paper for a mental health publication about this surprising and productive collaboration.

"I still have the paper that he wrote," Gregorio said. "It was not meant to be super scientific; it was meant for other psych techs, to illustrate the injection of optimism."

Yes, optimism was running high, but of course there were incidents. Some patients acted out in public, and others never fit in. Local doctors, many of them longtime family practitioners, were leery about getting involved with the treatment of these newcomers. In response, Gregorio and Haydee and the hospital staff spearheaded the idea of sending traveling teams, consisting of one or more psychiatrists, psychologists, nurses and psychiatric technicians, to work within the local medical communities and oversee the dispersal of medications. They urged local doctors to become involved and promised to be there when needed: "At any time we'll answer your calls and come to meet you." Gradually, said Gregorio, "The more sensitive general practitioners started to see this as a nice development."

Washington took notice too. Under the Kennedy administration, a Community Health Center Act authorized a grant-sharing program to establish localized mental health centers in small communities around the country. Relatively poorer regions (like Gregorio's Southeast Division) qualified for up to 90 percent funding by the federal government, ten percent by the local community.

All seemed to be going well. Then trouble, ever the unexpected guest, came knocking.

~

The old guard at the hospital had been swept from power, but they still had a lot of scrappy fight in them, and soon they lit on a powerful weapon: They rustled up support to launch a grand jury investigation. Their target was the unprecedented goings-on at the Colorado Mental Hospital and its unorthodox leader, Dr. Willis Bower.

Dr. Bower's enemies stirred up a disturbing scenario that went something like this: The stately old institution had thrown open the doors (and the windows and ceilings too, to hear some tell it), and now dangerous and deranged people were spilling from everywhere out onto the street and into neighborhoods and homes. Surely this new superintendent should be investigated for endangering the public...perhaps he should even face criminal charges!

In keeping with his controlled demeanor, Dr. Bower took his grand jury summons in stride. Haydee recalled how he gathered his staff together to explain the summons and how he would respond to it. "He went to the grand jury with an attitude like, 'I'm going to the supermarket today.' He was a good leader and a very well qualified therapist, and completely confident. He said, 'I can defend what we're doing.'"

Gregorio and Haydee, who were not called to testify, admired the way their boss tackled all the negative publicity and legal pressure with equanimity. It recalled for them the promise he made when they were hired: *"Either we make history or we fall flat on our faces."*

The grand jury challenge marked that razor-thin moment between triumph and failure. But the prescient Dr. Bower was unfazed. During his meeting with staff he made another promise, Haydee recalled. "He reassured all of us on the professional staff, 'We will fight this and we will win.'"

The day Dr. Bower testified, Gregorio and Haydee were there. They recalled the atmosphere in the room—"It wasn't friendly at all"—and the grim edginess of the opposition witnesses, which was all too obvious from their flat stares and the angry set of their jaws. They made their case in broad and emotional strokes, Gregorio recalled. "They presented it as, 'The patients are a danger, they're going to attack us, they want to ruin the community...' It was not very sophisticated testimony."

Then it was Dr. Bower's turn. Calmly but forcefully he explained the reasoning and the careful, step-by-step approach that buttressed the concept of geographic decentralization. He explained how the plan, radical as it seemed, would prove to be a boon for patients, for the field of mental health, and for all the citizens of Colorado. People who needed customized care would continue to get it, and good people who had been shunted into the shadows would have the opportunity to live full lives again, reunited with their families and communities. The world was ready for this innovation, thanks to psychiatric advancements of the day which included modern drug treatments, behavioral and medical therapies, and the enlightened training of support staff. Human beings once locked helplessly behind closed doors could contribute to the world once again. No longer would they live out their lives known as "patients," but rather as "productive citizens."

As Dr. Bower talked, the Korts sensed a subtle change coming over the room. "The judge in particular was really impressed," Gregorio recalled. Dr. Bower had managed to shift the atmosphere from fear to hope. Later, in the final grand jury report, it was clear Dr. Bower had persuaded the presiding judge. As Gregorio put it, "He was impressed with the progress that was going to be made, as opposed to the danger everyone *thought* was going to happen."

In retrospect, Gregorio and Haydee believe the grand jury investigation turned out to be a very positive thing for the Colorado State Hospital, and scrutiny of its groundbreaking work actually strengthened the cause.

"It was a really good thing because in the grand jury room, the concept of geographic decentralization was put on the table and looked at from every angle without biases," Gregorio said. "The community was able to have its say, and so was the superintendent. All questions and concerns were addressed and then put to sleep."

Haydee added, "People saw that the result wasn't danger, it was progress."

In the end, as Dr. Bower promised, he had won over the opposition, and perhaps even turned some former enemies into supporters. Said Gregorio: "We were all proud to be in this community where psychiatric history was being made."

They had weathered internal opposition, community suspicion, logistical challenges and a towering obstacle course that involved relocating thousands of patients throughout the state.

Perhaps now there would be smooth sailing for the hospital? Perhaps Gregorio and Haydee could return to the absorbing work that had brought them to Colorado, to work alongside Dr. Bower, and help him run an innovative and finely tuned psychiatric institution.

In reality, the answer was complicated. First, to set their professional lives on course the two young psychiatrists had a major hurdle to overcome. They needed a Colorado medical license to continue to practice medicine in the state, and that meant an intense study period of six to nine months.

In Argentina, Gregorio and Haydee had fulfilled all their obligations to earn their medical degrees and enter residency programs in the USA. Once established in their new country, the Korts had passed all the required medical tests to practice medicine in America. So initially, when they arrived in Colorado, that was enough. Their new boss, Dr. Bower, was a pragmatist; he had hired them because he was impressed with their skills and understanding of modern psychiatric methods. The Colorado license? Yes, they could begin to study for it, but in the meantime Dr. Bower was pleased to have them working for him and the hospital.

So, in the midst of everything else—reorganizing an entire hospital, facing professional opposition, running a family (little Marcelo was barely a toddler), and finally, weathering a grand jury investigation—Gregorio and Haydee were still "students," studying for a final exam!

The fact that Dr. Bower was relaxed about when they obtained their Colorado licenses relieved a great deal of pressure for Gregorio and Haydee. Their family life was already packed, and just as important as their work at the hospital, so much so that Haydee's mother and father came from Argentina to help with Marcelo while his parents studied in their spare time.

As for Dr. Bower, he was results-oriented. He knew Gregorio and Haydee were excellent physicians who were legally able to practice medicine in the USA, and they produced results, so he didn't consider the exact timing of their Colorado medical exam as critical.

Then trouble doubled back, and this time there was nothing they could do to make it go away.

Dr. Bower quit.

~

The news came suddenly, like a sock in the eye. As so often happens in a crisis, the moments leading up to it were perfectly normal. One morning in 1963, Dr. Bower announced to his key staff members that he was resigning to become Director of Psychiatric Training at UCLA.

Gregorio and Haydee and the entire senior team were stunned into silence. The Korts had been in Pueblo for about two years; the decentralization plan had been in effect for about a year, and the new system was working well—thanks to the steady hands of Dr. Bower and Dr. Garcia. Now what?

"It felt like our father was deserting us," Gregorio said.

However, when they looked back, it was clear that Dr. Bower's professional goals did not end in Pueblo, Colorado. He had been summoned by the governor to take on the challenge of implementing geographic decentralization, an unprecedented and historic innovation in the field of mental health. He had revitalized the Colorado State Hospital and created a network of care for the mentally ill that was designed to last for years to come. He had found highly talented people, starting with Dr. Gregorio and Dr. Haydee Kort, to run it. Now it was time for him to move on.

"We think he decided a long time before that he was going to get this accomplished just as he promised the governor, and then he was going to leave," said Haydee, and Gregorio added, "He had accomplished his mission at the hospital, and in a positive way."

Once again, the future looked unpredictable at the Colorado State Hospital. Yes, Dr. Bower had brought in as Clinical Director the innovative Dr. Garcia, their trusted and talented mentor from Iowa, but he was facing his own professional pressures, many of them rising from his image as a "foreign-born" doctor in Pueblo. Meanwhile, Gregorio and Haydee each possessed an approachable temperament, which helped them blend easily into the community as both physicians and neighbors.

Now, just as they were feeling settled in their personal lives, once more their career paths were looking uncertain. However, Dr. Gregorio Kort and Dr. Haydee Kort always knew when to pause from the stresses at work to become Goyo and Beba again, and that was because they held fast to one personal rule: "Home by Five."

CHAPTER NINE

"HOME BY FIVE"

On any given evening, the staff who relied on Dr. Gregorio Kort and Dr Haydee Kort for their psychiatric expertise and clinical skills would have been charmed, and maybe surprised, to get a peek into the after-hours world they returned to every evening, a pretty ranch house at 3127 High Street.

There, they were likely to see Haydee busy at the stove, making dinner while little Marcelo caroused nearby. (Gabriela's birth was still to come, in 1963.) Meanwhile, Greg, as he was known to many people away from work, was backing the family Oldsmobile out of the driveway to take Marcelo's nanny/babysitter, Melba Stockwell, back to her home at the end of her long day's work.

This sweet world away from the Colorado State Hospital had begun at their rented home at 47 Caledonia Street, and continued when they bought their first home about nine months later on High Street. It was a comforting, stable, and deliberately homespun end to the workday, because for psychiatrists Gregorio and Haydee Kort, it was absolutely as important as the workday itself.

"We were fully aware that this was the life we wanted to have," Gregorio said. "The way I would describe it is that we made a conscious effort to balance work and life. It was not a hit-and-miss proposition. We were very conscious about trying to be home at five o'clock, and everything that went with having a family."

"That's why we didn't go into private practice," Haydee explained, "because there are no hours that are 'off limits' in a private practice, while at the hospital we could keep a schedule that permitted us to get home at five o'clock, at the latest five thirty, to be with the kids."

From the beginning, the Korts' professional careers were part of a family enterprise. Little Marcelo even came along on the long drive from Iowa when Gregorio and Haydee interviewed with Dr. Bower for the first time. Dr. Bower's staff arranged for babysitters to watch over Marcelo while his parents interviewed and toured the hospital campus. Not only did they bring their baby along to their Pueblo interview, but they made "home by five" a stipulation of their new jobs, and Dr. Bower readily agreed. To carve out more family time they had to take a stand, for example when the hostile assistant superintendent insisted that they work on Saturdays.

They won that battle, and from then on, the Korts were able to build a life that was as full and complete *away* from the Colorado State Hospital as in it. Prosaic duties like mowing the lawn? That they left to others, but family meals, enjoying friends, and most of all, being with Marcelo and Gabi (as she is called), were the bonds that created a fulfilling and busy life. For the Korts, the titles "Mom" and "Dad" were just as important as the titles "Doctor" and "Psychiatrist."

However, there is one foundational factor that makes their lifestyle work, and it has been a constant throughout their lives:

Then and now, Goyo and Beba have always been a team.

"We supported each other," Gregorio said, looking back. "That has always been a very important ingredient in our relationship. That doesn't mean we were always on a 'high' about everything, sometimes we were down. But we'd rehash whatever was bothering us and keep going."

"We were happy together," Haydee agreed. "And we liked what we were doing at work, and we were glad we were able to do it."

Yes, there was a fair amount of "office talk" around the family table; after all there's a lot to catch up on when husband and wife work in the same far-flung hospital system yet rarely see each other during the day. But at home, family always came first.

"Haydee wanted the full experience being a mother, to be seen by the children as their mother," Gregorio said. "So she didn't want the babysitter cooking dinner; she *wanted* to do it! So our goal was always when we get to the hospital we work; when we're home, it was, 'Let's be a family.'"

Two psychiatrists for parents. Surely that played a role in the raising of children? However, even in that regard, Gregorio and Haydee say they were careful to maintain a distance between their professional lives and their family. They used their instincts as parents, not as psychiatrists, to raise their kids. That said, they were strongly protective of their children.

"I'll tell you an anecdote," Gregorio said. "When Marcelo was ready to start pre-kindergarten, the mothers of his friends offered to include Marcelo in the carpool. They knew we couldn't reciprocate because we had to be at the hospital early in the morning.

"Anyway, we appreciated that, and we got to be very good friends with the mothers of the other children..."

The year progressed, Marcelo attended the Episcopal pre-school with his friends, and then it was time to move on to Morton Elementary School.

Gregorio smiled at the memory. "Haydee was talking to the mothers, asking if they were going to continue the carpool, but they said it was time the kids walked to school on their own. But she wanted to keep protecting him!"

At home and at work, when Haydee spoke, people listened—so the demise of the carpool wasn't taken lightly in the Kort household. But just like at work, there was no problem that one or both of the Drs. Kort could not solve. In this case, the answer was simple: When Marcelo walked to school with the others, the babysitter Melba Stockwell was tasked with following him at a distance from a block away to make sure he got to school safely.

Education of their children was incomparably important. In Argentina, academics were stressed and serious study was the norm, and that is what the Korts sought for Marcelo and Gabriela in America. Raised themselves in secular Jewish homes in Argentina, Gregorio and Haydee were not averse to sending Marcelo and Gabriela to a school with another religious tradition, like the Episcopal pre-school, as long as the standards were high. As they entered middle school and high school, the Pueblo public school system was thoroughly acceptable.

And as it turned out (to their chagrin), Gregorio and Haydee were not done with their own American education, either.

Yes, their medical degrees from Argentina had been fully accepted in the U.S., otherwise they could not have been accepted into hospital residency programs in Tennessee. Colorado was more stringent. They learned that the State Medical Board required that they obtain a license to practice medicine in the state. In the relatively relaxed bureaucratic requirements of the early Sixties, Dr. Bower had allowed the Korts (his two most trusted psychiatrists and closest allies) as much time as they needed to complete their studies.

Then suddenly, Dr. Bower, their champion and mentor, was gone. The new superintendent, Dr. Charles Meredith, was more strict. Gregorio recalled: "Dr. Meredith issued a directive that all the unlicensed physicians have only so much time to get their Colorado license *or else*. We knew that meant we would be out of a job."

The question was, how could they work full time, have a family life with Marcelo, and also study for this highly complicated medical exam which would determine their future?

Then, in a sweet turn of events—but to complicate the deadline even more—while they were studying for the exam, Haydee became pregnant with Gabriela. At the time, the family was still living in their small rented home on Caledonia Street. Although it was a tight fit, the solution to Gregorio and Haydee's latest professional challenge was to turn to family. Haydee brought her parents, Jose and Sofia Kantorovich, from Argentina to watch over Marcelo, while she and Gregorio literally retreated to the basement every night after work and on weekends to study for the exam.

"Study, study, study, that's all we had to do," Haydee recalled, with a smile. They were so focused that Haydee's parents brought their meals to them in the basement rather than disturb their concentration.

The influence of Grandpa Jose and Grandma Sofia turned out to be an excellent boon for little Marcelo. To this day Haydee and Gregorio recall with great fondness the sight of Haydee's father strolling through the Pueblo neighborhood on one of his daily walks, carrying little Marcelo in his arms.

"Marcelo was so happy with his grandparents," Gregorio said, smiling at the memories. "Jose, Haydee's father, would take him in his arms and go out in the neighborhood and make friends with the neighbors, especially a Spanish-speaking family that lived nearby. Marcelo was in heaven."

"Yes," Haydee added, "and he almost forgot English!"

In fact, Marcelo grew up to be effortlessly bilingual. And for Haydee to have her mother so close by was a comfort and a support during a stressful time.

∼

Meanwhile, Argentina, and the families and friends that Goyo and Beba left behind, were never far from their hearts. Even though the Colorado medical license exam was becoming a constant background noise in their lives, the young family (minus Gabriela, who was not born yet) was able to return to Argentina for an epic, month-long reunion that turned out to be both memorable and harrowing.

"Dr. Bower was very generous to approve our time away," Gregorio said. "It had been five years since we had seen any family member except Haydee's mother, who came to stay with us when Marcelo was born."

The visit was a joyful event with international flavor, featuring the two adventuresome psychiatrists from America with baby son Marcelo, and about twenty of their relatives: parents, siblings, cousins, uncles and aunts. The reunion began, and continued, on such a high note—"We were having a great time!" Gregorio said—that at some point the decision was made to head, en masse, for the sparkling resort city of Mar del Plata, a sunny playground of wide beaches and comfortable hotels located 260 miles south of Buenos Aires on the Atlantic coast.

Gregorio's sister Natalia had an apartment in Mar del Plata where everyone regrouped to continue the historic family gathering. There, the visit continued over many days, and all was as easy and sunny as the beaches squishing under their feet.

Until the night, that is, when Gregorio woke up in terrible pain.

"I felt it was appendicitis, and I quickly woke up my brother Moises who had a car," he continued. Lights blazed on, dazed sleepers struggled awake, and suddenly, the crowded and darkened apartment was buzzing with urgency and concern. *Gregorio needed help.*

Then came the mad dash for the car, as mad anyway, as a bent-over Gregorio could take it. That's when things went from bad to worse. When they got down to the street, the sickening truth was as obvious as the empty parking space: The car had been stolen.

Haydee sprang into action. She ran into the street and started to flag down cars. "We *had* to get a taxi or car to take him to the hospital!" At her side was Gregorio's older brother Marcos. These two desperate figures, wife and brother, waving their arms in the middle of the night, may have been the thin line between life and death for Gregorio, because he was clearly in bad shape. "By then I was ready to crawl to the hospital," he said.

A car stopped and they got to the hospital. Next task: Find a surgeon.

That's when the ever-resourceful Haydee had another idea. She had the presence of mind to remember that her former ballet teacher was married to a surgeon. (Imagine getting a call, in the middle of the night, from your former star pupil who had moved to America, who was now on the phone and desperate for help.)

"Her husband recommended somebody who could do the surgery in Mar del Plata and he did," Haydee recalled. "Greg barely made it, because it turned out his appendix was infected."

Like all averted tragedies, the event became a good story that ended in a much-appreciated anticlimax: Gregorio spent most of the reunion recuperating in bed, not luxuriating on the beach.

Yet their rich family traditions would include other beaches in Argentina, and other fond family memories. Gregorio's brother, Moises, bought a summer home closer to Buenos Aires where Haydee and a (healthy) Gregorio could share family time and the classic Argentinian barbecue called an *asado,* consisting of smoldering, sizzling, endless expanses of spicy chorizo sausage and short ribs on the grill. All of it was top quality because it came from Moises, who worked in one of Argentina's famous meatpacking plants and had access to only the finest.

Like a soft but persistent rain, the Korts' trips back to Argentina gently settled into the families' minds that Haydee and Gregorio were making America their permanent home. What had been, in the beginning, the families' grief at their departure, settled into resignation and finally acceptance, because Goyo and Beba's frequent vacations home assured everyone in Argentina that the American branch of the family would visit often, and never be away for long.

Of course, after the appendicitis caper passed into the family lore, the Korts endured endless teasing. Laughing, Gregorio recalled, "One of the family said, 'Are you sure you'll come back again to visit? Because after appendicitis and surgery and the complications we wonder if we'll see you again for twenty years!'"

~

When Gabriela (called Gabi) was born in 1963, her parents discovered just what kind of impact they had made on the hospital in less than three years.

"Haydee had an incredible relationship with the care staff, and they threw all kinds of baby showers for her, and they came to visit after Gabi was born," Gregorio remembered, still deeply affected, almost six decades later, by the outpouring of affection for his wife and newborn daughter. In the stressful and sometimes grim world of a mental hospital, the loyalty that the staff showed to Haydee at the birth of Gabi would resonate through the years.

For Marcelo and Gabi's parents, the birth of their daughter meant their family was complete. Two children were just right. Even sweeter, the hope had always been for a son *and* a daughter. "We were delighted," Haydee said, while Gregorio painted a picture of their happiness back in 1963 with a laugh and a fist pumped in the air: "We did it! We did it!"

Still ahead were the growing-up years, the boyhood explorations of Marcelo, and the tennis championships for Gabi; the world travels the family would take together; and yes, the outdoor adventures that Gregorio and Haydee would pioneer for the patients at the hospital in which their two children would participate as well.

But that was all ahead. In the meantime, another challenge loomed in the Korts' professional lives, and that challenge was adjusting to a new superintendent: Dr. Charles Meredith.

CHAPTER TEN

A NEW WAY OF DOING THINGS

Haydee was medical director of the Colorado Springs Division when she had a disturbing exchange with the newly appointed head of that city's community mental health center. The decentralization revolution was well underway and community mental health centers had become the norm. They were part of the legacy of the previous and highly innovative superintendent, Dr. Willis Bower.

Now a new man, Dr. Charles Meredith, was in charge, and Haydee was about to learn firsthand, "out in the field," that there was great suspicion about how the exciting concept of decentralization was going to fare under a new boss.

Amiably, Haydee introduced herself to the new director of the community mental health center, expecting to begin a productive conversation. Instead, he returned her friendly greeting with a wince of distaste. He told her that he didn't care who she was, but it seemed to him that, if Dr. Bower had resigned as superintendent, the future looked pretty bleak for decentralization.

Haydee, never known to back down from a challenge or a rebuff, replied briskly, "Well, I wish you'd take time to judge me not for what you *think* will happen but for what I'm going to do!"

As would become clear in later years, when Haydee spoke, people not only listened, they often changed their minds. So it happened with the community health director. "To make a long story short," Haydee continued, "we became the best of friends. He learned to like me and respect me and we worked together well."

However, their ominous opening exchange suggested that the new era, under the new superintendent, might not be easy.

According to Haydee and Gregorio, Dr. Charles Meredith was the choice of a search committee established by the Colorado Department of Institutions, Division of Mental Health. Dr. Bower was on the search committee too, and by then he was motivated to find his successor quickly. As Haydee put it, "He was done; he wanted to leave."

Dr. Charles Meredith, originally from Canada, was a psychiatrist. The search committee and the state of Colorado considered psychiatry a critical credential for a superintendent, but it wasn't considered particularly essential that the candidate be enthusiastic about the new movement called decentralization. As Haydee put it, "Dr. Meredith was well qualified in terms of his credentials, but he wasn't necessarily familiar with the things that the hospital was planning to do."

From the start, Dr. Meredith's actions made it clear that the post-Bower era had arrived. Fortysomething, self-assured, with sleek, swept-back hair and a confident grin, the new superintendent arrived with his wife and seven kids, and moved directly into the superintendent's mansion-like house on the hospital grounds.

In most places, his choice to live in the superintendent's house would have been natural. But his predecessor, Dr. Bower, had moved into one of the city's neighborhoods, which sent the message he wanted to be involved in the wider community of Pueblo. In the vast scheme of things, Dr. Meredith's choice of a home, more formal and traditional, wasn't a deal breaker when it came to his likeability, but it was clear that a new era had begun.

It also seemed that Dr. Meredith wanted to return at least some control to the traditional hospital hierarchy. Under Dr. Bower, Gregorio and Haydee were able to manage their own divisions and solve problems at their own level, and they were given authority above and beyond their own divisions to manage the other teams. "We were in charge of all the disciplines; we could even hire or fire if we needed to," Haydee explained.

By contrast, Dr. Meredith preferred the formal route of governance that began with the director of nursing and the other department heads, the system that was in the process of being dismantled under Dr. Bower. Now, under the new superintendent, Haydee said, "if there was a nursing problem in one of the divisions, Dr. Meredith would call the director of nursing…"

It was evident that two very different management styles were in play: Would control of the hospital consolidate under a traditional hierarchy again, or would decentralization continue?

Perhaps the most noticeable, immediate change under the new superintendent was that he stopped attending the both loved-and-dreaded daily meetings that Dr. Bower had established with the team leaders. Though Dr. Bower often put individuals on the spot ("You're going off topic, please stay on the point!" was one often-heard directive), the consensus was that the must-attend meetings kept the hospital staff motivated. By his absence, it became clear to Haydee and Gregorio and the rest of the staff that Dr. Meredith didn't enjoy those meetings and that he questioned their value. Inevitably, without his presence, the meetings lost their power.

Despite those changes, Dr. Meredith didn't force his new approach on the staff; in many ways, he let the new decentralization system roll on. And if he didn't offer the visionary enthusiasm and innovations of Dr. Bower, well, the staff would just have to supply that enthusiasm for decentralization themselves. As Haydee explained, "He didn't support it, and he didn't stop it either."

~

One bright spot (for a time anyway) was Dr. Luis Garcia-Bunuel, the Korts' friend and mentor from Iowa. In one of his major flourishes, Dr. Bower had hired Dr. Garcia as Clinical Director of the Colorado State Hospital and put Haydee at his side as Assistant Clinical Director.

In Colorado, the professional lives of the Korts and Dr. Garcia, their former Iowa boss, officially came full circle. Dr. Garcia, originally from Spain, was a welcome presence in Haydee and Gregorio's lives. His family, wife and kids, became great friends of the Korts as well. The two families spent happy hours in each other's back yards, grilling steaks and bantering away in Spanish, two professional families from immigrant backgrounds, brought together by fate to a small city in southern Colorado, USA.

If only the medical powers-that-be in Pueblo had been as fond of Dr. Garcia! In fact, he was an outsider who challenged conventional, old-guard thinking about mental health issues, and that made the insiders more than uneasy. Dr. Garcia was intensely supportive of decentralization and fearless about his belief that the needs of each mentally ill individual were a higher priority than the hospital bureaucracy itself.

"Well, he was pretty aggressive in how he presented himself," as Gregorio put it, "and the private-practice surgeons were not about to take that from a foreigner. So they cornered him to the point that he had to leave."

One surgeon went so far as to write a damaging and untruthful letter to the hospital board accusing Dr. Garcia of meddling in outside politics. Making things worse, one of the hospital administrators was also undermining Dr. Garcia, and as an insider, he had the means to do it. From the sidelines, Haydee and Gregorio watched these developments with alarm. Haydee was working alongside Dr. Garcia and saw it firsthand. Slowly but surely, Dr. Garcia was being pushed out. Was it hospital politics? Or was it his status as a foreigner?

In the highly charged politics of the state hospital system it was difficult to know, but one fact mitigated against the foreigner theory—after all, Haydee and Gregorio were foreigners too. Yet they felt themselves completely accepted in the hospital system and in the larger Pueblo community.

"It's kind of comical, you know, that people will tell us, 'Well, you know how some people think about foreigners,'" Gregorio said. "And then they'd turn to us and say, 'But we're not talking about you; *you* are different!'"

～

According to Haydee, the hospital insider who was pushing out Dr. Garcia disliked him and Dr. Meredith with equal fervor. By the same token, this insider was a champion of Haydee and saw her as the natural choice to take over as Clinical Director.

In the political labyrinth of the state hospital system, that is eventually what happened. Pueblo's medical community, led by a contingent of private-practice surgeons, made life uncomfortable for Dr. Garcia until he moved on to better things. Meanwhile, both Haydee and Gregorio continued to prosper in their chosen positions. Gregorio was head of the Southeast Division, where he could pursue his calling to work closely one on one with individual patients, and Haydee, an administrator at heart, was serving as Clinical Director of the entire hospital system.

Clearly, despite all the political upheavals at the hospital (the resignations, the complaints, and the carping), the Korts continued to prosper. To this day, they have no particular explanation for that. But others do. They observe that Gregorio and Haydee were universally regarded as genuine people and skilled psychiatrists who demonstrated authentic compassion and skill toward each mentally ill individual. They knew how to make friends and keep them. Colleagues liked them. In their professional work, they were reasonable and fair. In their private lives, people saw a devoted couple who loved their family.

However, into this thicket of happiness a thorn was about to snag their professional contentment: *the state medical license!* Dr. Bower's relaxed approach to the license problem ended when he left, and Dr. Meredith, his successor, issued a directive that the Korts only had a few months left to get their Colorado license, or they would have to go.

The Korts took on the challenge. They battened down the hatches in their book-strewn basement, finished their studies, and passed the rigorous exam. Their licenses were assured and they had no reason to think their troubles were anything but over.

That's when the proverbial roof caved in. Inexplicably, the State Board of Medical Examiners in Colorado refused to take the final step to approve their licenses, "even though we had passed the same tests," Haydee said, "and had received the same diploma as the others, and had been practicing in Colorado for several years!"

The reason? Gregorio explained: "They said our medical school degree in Argentina was not valid in Colorado."

~

What now? The Korts were aware that a foreign physician had never been granted a Colorado medical license. Their colleague, Dr. Garcia (perhaps sensing those real but invisible barriers), had not even attempted to apply, and left the state instead.

"We believed it was an excuse to get rid of the foreign doctors," Gregorio observed. However, by that time Gregorio and Haydee were committed to Colorado and to the Colorado State Hospital at Pueblo. Their careers were thriving except for the bureaucratic conundrum created by the State Medical Board, which did not dispute that the Korts had successfully passed the test to get their Colorado medical license. What the board *did* dispute was the validity of their medical degrees from Argentina.

How would the Korts untangle this rat's nest? By then they had been practicing medicine in the USA for nearly five years, and no hospital—not in Tennessee or Iowa, nor up to then, in Colorado—had questioned their degrees from Argentina.

The answer came from a most unlikely source: One of the surgeons who sat on the medical board itself.

"Sue the bastards," he said.

Did Gregorio and Haydee hear that right? The medical-board member repeated himself: "I know, I know, I'm one of them," he said. "But I'm telling you it's the only way you'll get anywhere. Sue us!"

No, he wasn't taunting the Korts; he was being helpful. He wanted them to succeed, and he felt they were being treated unfairly.

Gregorio and Haydee took his advice and hired a seasoned Pueblo lawyer, C. Todd Kettelkamp, to take their case.

As it turned out, the Korts had more than their lawyer and one maverick surgeon on their side. Their lawyer instructed them to round up as many prominent people as possible to testify on their behalf, and the list turned out to be impressive indeed: it included the director of the Colorado Springs Mental Health Center, the director of the State Hospital at Fort Logan, and the Chairman of the Department of Psychiatry at the University of Colorado.

Attorney Kettelkamp had a strategy. He figured he could get farther, faster—and without filing a lawsuit—just by imposing a little clever pressure on the medical-board bureaucrats. On the day of the hearing, a prominent pack of supporters gathered in Denver with Haydee and Gregorio outside the forbidding door of the Medical Board. Just before he was called into the meeting, Mr. Kettelkamp motioned them all together and explained what he was going to say to the obstructionists.

"Let me handle it," he said. "I'm going to go in there and explain that Gregorio Kort and Haydee Kort have the same qualifications as any medical professional in Colorado, and right outside this door I have ten highly qualified and prominent people waiting to speak to you who know the Korts and will convince you of their capabilities!"

And that's what the attorney did. The board was flustered. "We don't have time to listen to all those people!" they huffed, adding they had only one day to get through a long list of work items, and they had no time to listen to statements from ten people who weren't even on the agenda. That would take days, and it just wasn't going to happen!

That's when the tide began to turn. Was it the threat of nearly a dozen prominent people waiting just behind the door, eager to testify for their colleagues, that did it? Or maybe it was the not-so-veiled hints of a lawsuit from a clever Pueblo lawyer?

"The whole strategy," Gregorio explained, "was that our lawyer knew that the members of the State Board of Medical Examiners were private practitioners, surgeons and internal medicine physicians and so on, and none of them wanted to waste days and days listening to testimony on a bothersome foreign physician issue."

The upshot was that suddenly that very day, the medical school in Argentina was miraculously found to be in good standing by the Colorado Medical Board. A few minutes later, Mr. Kettelkamp stepped into the hallway where Gregorio and Haydee and their crowd of distinguished and renowned supporters waited.

"Your licenses are approved," he said. The dignified crowd erupted into decorous applause and a wave of congratulations.

"I cried," Haydee confessed. "I was so happy."

Gregorio and Haydee were also gratified and touched that nearly a dozen of Colorado's most prominent medical people, all institutional leaders at the top of their professions, had torn themselves away from their busy schedules for a day to come down to the State Medical Board to help them.

As for Dr. Meredith's role in the proceeding, he did not attend the hearing, but he did get what he had demanded: Gregorio and Haydee were officially in good standing with the state of Colorado. In the end, it took all of fifteen minutes and the Korts' medical careers in Colorado were assured.

The entire incident cost the Korts an attorney's fee of two thousand dollars (not a small sum in 1964) and also a special promise that Mr. Kettelkamp extracted from them, that they owed him a pricey bottle of Argentine wine '57.

To this day, Gregorio and Haydee marvel at the quick work of their clever lawyer, or as Haydee describes him, "The best lawyer in town!"

Nor has Mr. Kettelkamp let them forget it. It just so happens that the Korts and their lawyer live in the same neighborhood, and to this day, more than fifty years later, if Attorney C. Todd Kettelkamp happens to see Gregorio and Haydee strolling past his house, he always gives them a big wave and a shout, "When are you getting me that bottle of '57 wine from Argentina?!"

CHAPTER ELEVEN

"SOMETHING SIGNIFICANT HERE"

Gregorio and Haydee dodged a deep crevasse when the Colorado Medical Board approved their medical degrees from La Plata University Medical School in Argentina. Without that approval, they would have had to leave Colorado to continue their medical careers.

In a way, the ordeal with the State Medical Board gave their diplomas even more meaning than when they were earned in 1957. Said Gregorio, "They were obtained by a lot of sweat and blood…"

"…A *lot* of sweat and blood," Haydee agreed.

In 1963, with those hard-won medical diplomas officially honored in Colorado, the two Drs. Kort could pause and assess their future.

They had done the same kind of assessment two years before when they sat down in their shabby little Pueblo hotel room to review their first interview with the charismatic Dr. Bower. At the time, they had debated whether they really wanted to cast their futures with the Colorado State Hospital. Did they want to take on the challenges Dr. Bower laid out for them? He had promised they would make psychiatric history "or fall on our faces," and he added a prediction wrapped in a warning: "*I think we are going to do something significant here and make a big contribution to psychiatry, and if we don't, we'll all be looking for a job together!"*

They signed on anyway, and the result was a triumph-in-the-making. The decentralization plan was being accomplished *in spite of* all the challenges and opposition.

But now circumstances were different. Dr. Bower had gone on to find his next job. As Gregorio said, "When he left, it was like losing a good friend." Sure, Dr. Bower had been painfully frank about the challenges in Pueblo, but under his leadership he proved everything was possible.

Now the question was, were Gregorio and Haydee going to be able to continue that kind of work under his successor, Dr. Charles Meredith?

Under Dr. Meredith the hospital's challenges continued, but the new superintendent's style was to meet each event with cool, administrative aplomb. It was a very different style from Dr. Bower's fighting spirit and willingness to take on opposition aggressively. It was clear the decentralization movement still needed to be defended publicly, because whenever something went wrong at the hospital, anonymous leakers sprang to action to let the newspaper and the public know that decentralization was the villain. "We don't know specifically *which* people," Gregorio said, "but every so often if a patient escaped from the hospital, we were in the newspaper."

The mischief from the old guard, the displaced hierarchy, continued in the Meredith era. While it had technically lost power, the old guard was still a potent force both in the hospital and in the Pueblo community. The general unrest had helped to oust their friend and early supporter, Dr. Luis Garcia-Bunuel, and the way he was treated troubled the Korts: "We have a very big soft spot

for him as our mentor." Dr. Garcia's intense beliefs in what consti-
tuted quality patient care had turned people against him. Like Dr.
Bower, "He was a very strong believer that there's a need to treat
these patients like human beings and not like a bunch of people
locked up in a barn," Gregorio said. "You know, some people don't
take kindly to ideas like that."

So while invigorating innovations continued, there was also an
undertow of resistance and political intrigue at the hospital. Oddly
enough, although Dr. Meredith was the polar opposite of the intense Dr. Garcia in both manner and management philosophy,
many of the old-guard resistors didn't like either of them. "They
tried to make *both* Dr. Meredith's and Dr. Garcia's lives miserable,"
Haydee said.

Yet even when the Korts examined all the negatives, their career
path still pointed toward staying in Colorado. They had already
accomplished so much, and yes, they *had* made psychiatric history! As Gregorio put it, "The whole essence of the plan had already
been implemented and we were refining things, so we decided to
keep going with our jobs."

As it turned out, a high point was just around the corner for
the young couple from Argentina, because when Dr. Garcia left,
Haydee was named his successor as Clinical Director.

The news came as a happy surprise. Dr. Meredith may have
been less than enthusiastic about many aspects of decentralization, and he could have jeopardized the Korts' medical careers in
Colorado with his stern insistence on "following procedure" over
their medical licenses. Yet now he did something that showed
his support for the Korts' work. He appointed Haydee to take
over Dr. Garcia's responsibilities as Clinical Director and gave

the position a new name: Assistant Superintendent for Clinical Services.

Suddenly, Haydee had vaulted to the level of assistant superintendent, and even more important, she became one of the inner circle that reported directly to Dr. Meredith. And that wasn't all. In accordance with protocol, when Dr. Meredith was out of town, Haydee served as acting superintendent of the entire hospital system.

She was just 31 years old.

In her new roles as assistant superintendent and (when called upon) interim acting superintendent, Haydee had attained real power. "I was responsible for the functioning of the hospital and supervising the divisional heads, who included Greg and all the others."

In fact, not only was Haydee extraordinarily young, but she had become her husband's boss.

With a grin, Gregorio interjected, "Yes, and that gave a stability to my life. I had the same boss at work and at home!" In answer to a question he added, "This is interesting. It never crossed my mind, but many people have asked me over the years, 'How did you feel about being supervised by your wife?' And my answer has always been, 'She's better.'"

In other words, Gregorio explained, "She's better at that job than I would be."

If there is one key to explain the Korts' successful and lifelong careers, it may be the fact that they possessed entirely different but complementary skill sets. What's more, they *recognized* the complementary nature of their teamwork, and that energized their professional lives. They weren't compelled to compete with each other because they were each exercising their own talents exactly as they wanted to—Gregorio, by practicing psychiatry directly with individual patients, and thereby impacting the life of each person for the better; and Haydee, by managing the system and making policy decisions that impacted residents and the future of mental health practices throughout Colorado.

An added benefit was that they were also able to keep a hand in each other's skill set, Gregorio, by managing the Southeast Division and having a supervisory role over the other divisions, and Haydee, by continuing to work with patients and staff at an administrative level.

Of course, their extraordinary teamwork was based on their personal relationship and the trust and reliance they had in each other's judgment. Back in the early days of medical school, the youthful Haydee, just 17 years old, relied on Gregorio's help to adjust to the crushing study schedules and the difficult clinical work. In Pueblo, Haydee and Gregorio relied on their mutual teamwork as they both rose through the ranks to take on more responsibilities at the hospital.

Haydee explained, "Even though on paper I supervised Greg, in fact he helped me a lot and he gave me a perspective that no one else could. So somehow, I just went up the ladder. I was given the opportunity, and although I ended 'higher up,' so to speak, it didn't affect our relationship. I would say, 'If you had this situation, what would you do?' And he would help me with it."

On a professional level, Haydee had stepped into a rarified world of managers and administrators that still admitted few women at the time, "and I was very much aware of that."

Other things were moving forward too. On a positive note, the decentralization plan had created six independent divisions that by that time were running well, and Dr. Meredith wasn't impeding the natural leadership and innovative qualities of the Korts to continue that process. Meanwhile, the staff were excited to be part of many positive changes for the mentally ill, and they continued to gravitate to the Korts for direction and motivation.

"They were with us," Haydee said.

So the Pueblo Geographical Decentralization plan continued. One innovation that had begun under Dr. Bower but was fully implemented only after his departure was both historically significant and profoundly enlightened: It called for the separation of developmentally disabled persons from those who were mentally ill.

"One of the tasks we had as clinicians was to re-diagnose all the patients, and by doing that we discovered that there were five hundred patients who were in the developmentally disabled category," Gregorio said.

In other words, those five hundred people suffered from the kind of brain damage and brain injuries that used to be classified in the woefully misguided phrase, "mentally retarded." While it's impossible to make categorical pronouncements about the complexities of human psychology and psychiatry, a general idea helps explain how the developmentally disabled are different: They suffer physiological injuries to their physical *brains,* whereas the mentally ill suffer in their *minds,* which are two different kinds of human suffering.

In the outmoded mental health system that was developed in

the 1880s, people who inhabited these two different universes were not only treated the same, but they were thrown together side by side, though they had essentially nothing in common except their inability to live independently in society and to communicate effectively with others. In other words, under the old system, a person with severe cerebral palsy and a person with schizophrenia might be consigned to the same state hospital for the "insane," and they might share a ward together, but they did not share each other's worlds. The ongoing tragedy was that neither of them received the kind of treatment and attention that were specific to their needs.

With the breakup of the old system and the coming of new and enlightened leadership, all that changed, and Dr. Bower was among the first to recognize this. In one of his most forward-thinking acts before he resigned, Dr. Bower called for a new, separate institution for the five hundred individuals who had been diagnosed as developmentally disabled.

"He made such a persuasive case that there was no question that the legislature had to create a new school for the developmentally disabled," Gregorio said. That was done, and a new director was named for the developmentally disabled and a separate institution was formed.

Despite some resistance, the modernized system begun under Dr. Bower continued to flourish. The six thousand patients had been re-categorized. Traveling teams of psychiatric professionals fanned out across the state to meet with local community mental health staff about the needs of former hospital residents now living in their communities. On a federal level, Congress OK'd the Community Health Act, which sent tax dollars to impoverished regions of the country to pay for 90 percent of mental health needs in those communities, among them Gregorio's Southeast Division. Psychiatric technicians became a newly recognized category of mental health professionals, and training plans were created that allowed them to go to school, because a nationwide nursing shortage had created a special need. "We had to do something to get a stable staff, you know," Haydee said. "So one thing that was established, any psych tech that wanted to go to nurse's training could do that at full pay, at half their work schedule."

In that ten-year span from the mid-1960s to the mid-1970s, even some broken fences were mended. Perhaps the most unusual fence-mend was the outcome of Haydee's clash with the director of nursing who had resigned during the Bower era.

Yes, she had resigned, but she did not go away. One day, Haydee arrived for a hospital event, and there, across the room, stood her old nemesis.

The two approached each other (a polite greeting was clearly appropriate) and that's when the former nursing director said something startling and humbly gracious: "She came up to me and said, "Dr. Kort—I know I never called you Dr. Kort before, but I want to tell you, nobody ever had the guts to tell me the things you told me."

A memorable moment, all the more for coming out of the blue.

~

Over the next ten years, at least to the general public, the decentralized Colorado State Hospital system settled in as the new status quo. It was a little like a new family that rolls into the neighborhood and makes everyone uneasy, but over time becomes accepted, even likable.

Then in 1976-77 an internal shake-up began that would affect both the leadership of the Colorado State Hospital and the companion facility at Fort Logan, located in metro Denver. Dr. James Dolby, Director of the Colorado Division of Mental Health, contacted Haydee and said: "You need to help us…you need to come and run the Fort Logan Hospital."

At first blush, it looked like a great honor, but there were strings attached. Fort Logan was 130 miles away in Denver, and that meant Haydee would have to commute Monday through Thursday from Pueblo, a city the Kort family (including their two kids, Marcelo and Gabi) had come to love and didn't want to leave.

But Dr. Dolby gave Haydee no choice: She was going to Fort Logan as acting superintendent. Period.

Haydee stayed in Fort Logan for three months, and did such a good job of reinvigorating the staff and implementing new ideas that Dr. Dolby and the Division of Mental Health offered the Fort Logan position to her permanently, in no uncertain terms. Once again, she was backed against a wall: "They told me I don't have a choice."

Haydee and Gregorio conferred with each other and then drew in Marcelo and Gabi for a family conference. *"Listen, this is a serious position, we want to tell you about it…"*

In their hearts, the two Drs. Kort already knew what was best for their family. Haydee said, "We didn't want to live in Denver, and the kids wanted nothing to do with moving to Denver, and we respected that."

With that, Haydee, with regret and sadness, resigned from the

Colorado State Hospital where she had played a central role for fifteen years. "I felt it was time to do something else."

So she did. She quickly found a job as Director of the Spanish Peaks Mental Health Center, a Spanish-speaking organization that served Pueblo's large local Hispanic population, and was part of the community-based mental health system Haydee and Gregorio had helped to implement.

It looked like Haydee had made her next career step. Then one day, the phone rang.

Two men who shaped the future of Drs. Haydee and Gregorio Kort. (l to r); Dr. Luis Garcia-Bunuel and Dr. Willis Bower

The Kort Room came as a big surprise to Haydee and Gregorio when they retired in 1990. Here they are in 2018 with hospital historian Nell Mitchell, who created the Kort Room with her husband, Bob, and many staff.

Hospital unveils "Kort Room"

A tribute to Haydee Kort, M.D., "The Kort Room," was displayed recently at the Colorado State Hospital (CSH) Museum/Conference Center. The room is dedicated to Dr. Kort for her outstanding leadership and commitment to the highest quality of patient care.

Nell Mitchell, who developed the room, said the permanent wall display is a biography of Dr. Kort's career at CSH, serving as a record of her accomplishments that brought the hospital to its national number one standing. The biographical material traces Dr. Kort's background, her entry into hospital administration, and her major accomplishments and awards.

Among the clippings, awards, plaques, and other memorabilia, a stained glass transom from a long-since-gone hospital building is hanging. After years in storage, the transom was brought to Ms. Mitchell's attention by property manager Roy Crill. Ms. Mitchell rescued the artwork from obscurity when she and her husband, Bob, spent two weekend afternoons scraping and cleaning to reach the beauty underneath the layers of paint. She could see that the dusty transom of the 20's was a replica of today's sunburst logo of the Division of Mental Health.

On the wall of the Kort Room, a roundup of praise for Haydee's leadership in the banner year 1988

Superintendent Haydee Kort in her office (1980's)

The Kort Room keeps the legacy alive for future generations

The old telephone switchboard at the Colorado State Hospital: Where the many people seeking help for loved ones or themselves first made contact.

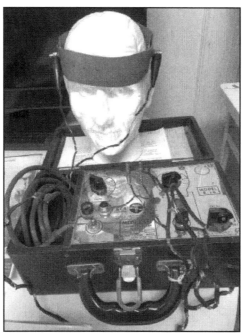

An early electroshock machine used at the Colorado State Hospital. First used in the late 1930's, electroshock treatments have undergone many technological improvements and to this day are an effective tool in treating certain cases of mental illness.

Charismatic and innovative, Dr. Willis Bower began the groundbreaking
decentralization process with Gregorio and Haydee Kort by his side

Dr. Charles Meredith

Dr. Haydee Kort, the 7th Superintendent of the Colorado State Hospital and the first woman to hold the position. Under her leadership the hospital became nationally recognized for its pioneering work to improve the lives of individuals suffering from mental illness.

A gallery of superintendents. During their tenures, the hospital changed its name to reflect the times: From the Colorado State Insane Asylum (1879-1899) to the Colorado State Hospital (until 1990) and finally to the Colorado Mental Health Institute at Pueblo (CMHIP), the name it holds to this day.

Gregorio and Haydee Kort in 2018, visiting the Hospital Museum developed by Nell and Bob Mitchell. The Kort Room occupies one wing. The building was the former superintendent's house. During her tenure as superintendent, Haydee resisted efforts by state officials to have it razed.

Dr. Haydee Kort with the plaque at the entrance to the Administration Building, which commemorates her years as Superintendent of the Colorado State Hospital

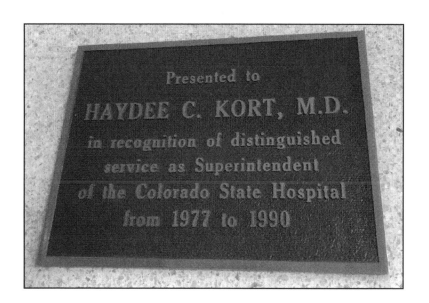

CHAPTER TWELVE

"MY LOVE WAS THE HOSPITAL"

The phone call came on a late fall afternoon in 1977, just as Haydee was getting ready to head home from her new office at Spanish Peaks Mental Health Center. She had been the center's medical director for only a few months.

A lot was riding on that unexpected call, and the proposal to Haydee that came with it. If Haydee could be drawn back to the fold as top administrator and Gregorio was free to introduce more innovations at the patient level, then the hospital could complete the historic revolution in patient care first envisioned in Clarinda, Iowa, in the late 1950s.

In fact, the call marked the beginning of the Kort legacy of leadership at Colorado State Hospital.

The caller was Dr. James Dolby, head of the Colorado Division of Mental Health, and that day he was an impatient man on a mission. The state had tried to convince Haydee to come to Denver and take over the Fort Logan Hospital permanently, and she had refused. But Dr. Dolby and the administrators in Denver weren't giving up. The state's mental health powers-that-be (in Pueblo, the hospital collectively referred to as "Denver") had taken notice of Haydee Kort's leadership qualities and her commitment to decentralization, staff empowerment and individualized patient care. Now a confluence of events made it even more important to bring Haydee back into the system.

"Haydee, we are offering you the position of superintendent of the Colorado State Hospital," Dr. Dolby said. He explained that after thirteen years in Pueblo, Dr. Meredith was planning to move on to his next career opportunity, and the superintendent position was open. Haydee was not only the right woman for the job ahead, but she was the right *person* for the job ahead, and Dr. Dolby hoped she would accept the position as soon as possible.

The news came "out of the blue," Haydee said. When she turned down the offer to run the hospital at Fort Logan and chose to resign instead, she figured she had cut her ties with the Colorado State Hospital for good. Now the future of the hospital system itself was being handed back to her in full.

"I'm very pleased to be offered the position, and I believe I am capable of doing the job," Haydee replied, "but I need to talk this over with my family, and of course with the people here, at Spanish Peaks, because they thought—and *I* thought—I was going to stay there forever!"

In fact, Haydee had already resolved that she could never come back to the Colorado State Hospital unless there was a way to fully implement the decentralization movement envisioned when she and Gregorio came to Pueblo in 1961.

The Korts knew full well that Dr. Meredith's leadership style was administrative, while they favored a more collaborative approach with staff, patients, and the community. They believed their hands-on approach was essential if a decentralized mental health system was ever to be fully integrated into the community at large.

Now in one phone call, Haydee was being assured that the field was cleared, and years of frustration over what *could* be accomplished for the mentally ill was resolving itself. Even though the hospital staff had pushed through as many innovations as possible in previous years, which included the years when Haydee was assistant superintendent, "There was much more to do."

This was her opportunity. "Can you let me know in a week?" Dr. Dolby asked.

One week! In fact, a deluge of reaction was building long before the week was out, and all of it was pushing Haydee in one direction, beginning with her family. When Haydee got home that night and told Gregorio the news, his reaction was immediate.

"Take it! Take it!" he said. Today, Gregorio's eyes still light up remembering the moment, because of the honor to Haydee, and because it resolved so many worries and unknowns. After Haydee had resigned from the hospital, Gregorio continued to run the Southeast Division of the hospital system as head psychiatrist, but as long as Haydee was working elsewhere, the Korts' lifelong goal of working together as a psychiatric team remained unfulfilled.

But if Haydee came back…!

As for the kids? Intergenerational harmony might be a rare commodity in many families, but not for the Korts. They were all in complete agreement. The whole family was united in their love for Pueblo. Marcelo and Gabi had formed deep friendships at school and through their many sports and extracurricular activities, and they did not want to leave. Their commitment was equally matched by their parents, who cherished the unique bonds that their children had formed, which they knew would be difficult to replicate in a new city. "One of the things no parent can really control or plan for," Gregorio explained, "is a situation where their kids have friends who are both fun loving and very good academically, and who come from families who have responsible positions in the community. We didn't want to disrupt that, and we thanked our lucky stars that our kids were hanging around with a very good group of kids."

More delicate was Haydee's relationship with the Spanish Peaks Mental Health Center, which she had joined as medical director only a few months before. "It was very tough," Haydee said. She already felt a loyalty to her new professional colleagues, and in fact, she felt indebted to them. As Gregorio explained, "After Fort Logan, when she was looking for a job, the Spanish Peaks people came through for her and they put all their money on her prestige and her abilities."

"So I was being pulled by one and the other, the hospital *and* Spanish Peaks, but my loyalties were still with the hospital," Haydee said.

While pressure was bearing in from both sides, it proved to be an affectionate and forgiving pressure. At the Colorado State Hospital, "They liked me, so they put pressure on me to take it," Haydee said. "And at the Spanish Peaks Mental Health Center, they understood too. They knew my loyalties were to stick with the hospital."

If there was any lingering fog of hesitation, it evaporated when support began pouring in from medical and mental health professionals across the state, including from the most influential quarter of all: "Haydee got a call from the Chairman of the Department of Psychiatry at the University of Colorado Medical School, offering its support," Gregorio said. "He told her to take the job, that whatever she needed they would support her and they would help her."

Encouragement poured in from every direction. "It was a conspiracy!" as Gregorio put it, with a grin. The institutional leadership of the state hospital system, the community mental health centers, the state medical board, already knew her record as psychiatrist, clinical director, and assistant superintendent. Most recently, they knew what she had done at Fort Logan as acting superintendent, and she had done it in a very short period of time. "What Haydee was able to do," Gregorio said, "was empower people throughout the hospital at Fort Logan, get their support, and make it a cohesive functioning hospital."

For Haydee herself, the decision to leave Spanish Peaks Mental Health Center so quickly was "a terrible decision to make." However, as she weighed her future at each institution, Haydee's instincts always turned, like the pull of a compass, in one direction.

"My love was the hospital," she said.

Haydee's tenure as superintendent of the Colorado State Hospital began on a high note. "There was no real adjustment for the hospital community," Gregorio pointed out. "Haydee already had a good record of defending and working with the staff. So when she took over, there were no negative vibes."

In fact, many staff members at the Colorado State Hospital made no secret of their loyalty to the Korts, and some even went to extraordinary lengths to try to keep her. Gregorio chuckled as he recalled when Haydee was getting ready to leave the hospital system for Spanish Peaks, some staff even cooked up an elaborate scheme to lobby for Haydee to remain at the hospital.

Their scheme turned on the fact that some members of the State Medical Board also happened to be the personal physicians for members of the hospital staff. Gregorio said these staff were so concerned about losing Haydee, "that they fabricated reasons to make appointments for medical checkups with their doctors who were also on the state board. They weren't making appointments to get a checkup; they wanted to use the time to tell their doctors to keep Haydee! It was a very cute, a very touching thing."

As for Gregorio, he recalled the good-natured teasing he took from colleagues about his "new boss." However, those jibes were easy to deflect because "Haydee is a better administrator than I am," as he told his colleagues, while his first love was the clinical care of patients. With Haydee at the helm, they could each do the work they loved best.

Within a few weeks of that fate-changing phone call from Dr. Dolby, Haydee was sworn in to the office of superintendent of the Colorado State Hospital system by U.S. District Judge Richard D. Robb. Judge Robb's wife, Patricia Robb, was a prominent attorney and assistant attorney general in the appellate division. She became a close colleague of Haydee's, and represented a number of state institutions including the Colorado State Hospital (renamed in 1990 as the Colorado Mental Health Institute at Pueblo).

Relationship building—whether with a prominent attorney or, for example, an influential newspaper editor—turned out to be one of Haydee's most notable strengths. Indeed, before "networking" even entered the lexicon, Haydee was an expert at it. One of her first acts as superintendent was to create a Community Mental

Health Advisory Board. She had long been concerned that there was a gulf between the workings of the Colorado State Hospital and the rest of the state and, most immediately, the citizens of Pueblo. She resolved to change that "us versus them" mentality and invite the outside world into her plans for helping the mentally ill in Colorado.

She and Gregorio had seen the damage that secrecy caused when a state institution turned off communication with the public and its more influential citizens. "So one of her first goals was to improve the relationship with the newspaper," Gregorio said.

When Haydee took the hospital reins, the 109-year-old *Pueblo Chieftain* was already a powerful voice in the community, a shaper of public policy since its founding in 1868. Unfortunately for the hospital, the newspaper's voice was often unfriendly when it came to hospital matters, especially in those rare but inevitable cases when there was a patient escape. In a notorious case in June 1974, ten patients hacksawed their way out of "Old Max 114" (a hospital building, clearly "maximum" in name only). According to hospital history, it took a month to round up all ten escapees, and the breakout eventually led to the building's closure. Such rare cases stirred up the public's imagination and alarm, and provided grist for the newspaper's ire. But apparently it didn't take outrageous cases like that to stir up the *Chieftain:* With a wry smile, Haydee said, "They blasted *anything* that happened at the hospital!"

One of her first invitations was extended to Bob Rawlings, the Chairman and Editor of the *Pueblo Chieftain.* She quickly followed up with prominent Pueblo businessman Bob Jackson, who owned a popular Chevy dealership and was a former Colorado state legislator. More legislators, business owners and influential policy makers followed, and they began to meet regularly, about every month. The program was a success, both practically and as a relationship-builder, Haydee said. "It was an opportunity for me to tell them about my plans for the hospital and any problems that had developed."

Problems? Within weeks, a problem developed that cast a cloud over Haydee's first year as superintendent. On a scale of seriousness, this problem was bad enough to make or break a career.

∼

Once again, Haydee's fortunes turned on a phone call from Dr. Dolby at the State Medical Board. Just a few weeks into her tenure he called to say he had a disturbing matter to discuss with her and it could not wait.

The ugly truth tumbled out quickly: The Colorado State Hospital was $3 million in the red! Worse, the shortfall had to be corrected before July 1, 1978, which was the start of the new fiscal year and only a short four months away.

"I wanted to die," Haydee said. (Accounting for inflation, the value of a $3 million deficit in 1977 is equivalent to a $12.5 million shortfall, four decades later.) But no matter how the amount was stacked, it was virtually insurmountable to overcome in four months, and would likely involve widespread program cutbacks, employee layoffs, and a furious union ready to do battle.

Dr. Haydee Kort had always been known for her even temper and a controlled and effective way of managing people and crises, but this news called for some raised decibels, and Haydee used them. Before she was hired, she told Dr. Dolby, "You should have leveled with me!"

"Well, that was part of the mess we were in," she recalled him saying.

"That answer didn't satisfy me. I was very mad," she said.

When she got home that night, her anger was still at full throttle. From the safety of fifty years gone by, Gregorio provided a colorful detail: "I didn't know she knew that many curse words!"

When her shock and surprise dissipated, Haydee took stock. The truth was, she had already accepted the position of superintendent, and now she was stuck. "Now I *had* to do the job, no matter what."

Haydee assessed her position (dire) and her options (nearly nonexistent). Then, once again, her instinct for relationship-building kicked in.

She called in the union.

If there is a dictionary example of a classic adversarial relationship, "management v. union" is a top contender. That was certainly the case at Colorado State Hospital. In fact, just a few years before, there had been a serious employee strike that left lingering memories. But that was just a dust-up compared to the union's expected reaction to a $3 million cutback, which for Haydee was an undeserved crisis that she had merely inherited.

Nevertheless, she forged ahead. "I knew I had to get close to Kathy Bacino, the union leader," Haydee recalled. "She was a very, very capable person, and I asked her to meet with me."

The two powerful women leaders met in Haydee's office in the administration building. Haydee recalled that she didn't want to waste time getting to the point, and she had no qualms about laying her cards on the table. She told Kathy Bacino: "Look, I don't usually tell the union something before I tell my own staff," she said, but now she needed the union's help. "I'm going to level with you," she said. "This is where we're at, and you are going to have to help me.'"

"You are asking us to do something against our own self-interest," Haydee recalled the union leader replying, in words to that effect.

Haydee pressed on. She laid out everything: the full shortfall, the looming deadline, the need to work together.

Looking back today, Haydee recalled the razor-thin path she was forced to walk: "Without the union I knew I was going to be in real trouble because in order to make up the three million dollars we had to do away with jobs," Haydee recalled. She told the union leader that her deadline to fix the budget was June 30, the end of the fiscal year.

"All of us are going to be affected by this," she told Ms. Bacino. "There is no other way but to make up this amount of money before June 30, and this is February!"

Haydee laid out the number of employees and wards that would have to be closed in order to make up the shortfall. However, there was an outside chance, "*If* we can work together," the superintendent told the union boss. If they could, jobs might be saved and they might weather the storm, but only if they were on the same team and not fighting each other.

Haydee's gift for blunt-spoken honesty and transparency built a new bridge that day. Kathy Bacino readily agreed to help. Recalling the crisis, Gregorio observed, "It was a very good example that if you can work with people you can avoid a crisis. It was a beautiful example of bipartisanship."

Still, they had an enormous amount of work to do. Kathy Bacino set the tone of the coming challenge by addressing her union membership with an urgent message: "We have no choice, this crisis isn't Dr. Kort's fault, she inherited it!"

Haydee and her team, which now included an unlikely ally, assessed the obstacles ahead. Some jobs could be eliminated by attrition. However, some wards, inevitably, would have to be closed. As much as possible, the important thing to avoid was closures that would create anguish in the community.

And that's when, immediately, Haydee's near-prophetic understanding for the need of a Community Mental Health Advisory Board paid off. Two members of the board were legislators who served on the legislature's Joint Budget Committee. Through their influence, the committee appropriated emergency funds that sopped up a part of the $3 million in red ink. It was only a stopgap measure, but it bought the hospital some time and gave hope.

Years later, Haydee could look back and smile at those tense but somehow exhilarating days. In the midst of catastrophe, she was uncovering skills that even *she* didn't know she had, especially when it came to playing the both delicate and brutal game of politics.

"Haydee really showed her skills dealing with the legislature," Gregorio said. "For example, she told them, 'Yes, I will cut the budget, but don't tell me *where* to cut—that's *my* job.'"

On the other hand, she knew instinctively that the best way to save programs and people was to allow the legislators, not herself, to take both the heat and the credit. After all, perception was critical, and Haydee knew that in this case, the elected representatives of the people would cut a more sympathetic figure than the institution that had created the mess. And that's how she lobbied the lawmakers: "If you, as legislators, fight for the programs, that will have a completely different outcome than if *I* fight for them," she told them.

Years later, Haydee reflected on how well she learned the sleight of hand that politics required. "Yes," she agreed, with a laugh, "it *was* clever of me—kind of sneaky!"

The legislators were playing the game, too. She recalled how one of the lawmakers, a member of her advisory committee, coached her before she testified before the Joint Budget Committee. "Now, I'm gonna have to give you a hard time when you testify," he warned her, "but don't worry, I'm on your side, I just have to play the game."

One potential source of public outrage was a proposal to close one of the children's cottages.

Most of Colorado was unaware that a small segment of the hospital population included minor children who suffered from mental illnesses and serious behavioral challenges. Those who were not able to return to their families were housed in small cottages on the hospital grounds. Their presence was not highly visible, and this was largely by design to protect their identities. But if a children's cottage was closed because of budget cuts? Well, in the public's mind, that would be the equivalent of an evil landlord throwing a family into a blizzard on Christmas Eve!

As she had proved by inviting the union to work alongside her, rather than against her, Haydee's shrewd leadership skills once again averted a public outcry.

At one of her Community Advisory Board meetings, Haydee recalled the scene. "Denver—the Division of Mental Health—wanted us to close one of the children's cottages. Bob Rawlings, the newspaper editor, asked me, 'Haydee, do you need that children's program?' I said, 'Of course we do!' He said, 'Let me have the phone in your office. I'm gonna call the governor, and tell him that if he cuts money from the children's program I'll blast him in the newspaper!'"

Not only did Haydee have the powerful voice of the newspaper working in her behalf, but she had a card to play that was largely hidden from view. The children's cottages were supported from separate grants and outside funding sources, and therefore were not technically on the $3 million chopping block. But it would not hurt to leave the impression with the public that in spite of the budget catastrophe, the children's programs had been preserved at all costs. Besides, Gregorio pointed out, under almost any scenario the public would back Haydee's protection of the children's programs. "Haydee knew that the community was very receptive to assume responsibility for treatment of children."

Few people begin a new job so universally respected and loved as Haydee Kort, only to be pulled into a disaster that could have destroyed her tenure almost before it began. Instead, it became a textbook example of Haydee Kort's "finest hour."

By the beginning of the 1978 fiscal year, the $3 million disaster had been averted. The legislature approved the new fiscal year budget for the hospital and some laid-off staff were even hired back. In less than a year, the confident 42-year-old psychiatrist and administrator had made the job her own.

And the Kort legacy was just beginning.

CHAPTER THIRTEEN

"LET'S SEE WHAT WE CAN DO!"

The decisive and powerful superintendent who averted a budget disaster and a potential labor strike in 1977 lived in a very different world from the two young psychiatrists who visited the Colorado State Hospital in 1961. In the course of that long-ago job interview, Haydee and Gregorio Kort had witnessed a heartbreaking sight:

On their first tour of the premises, they saw patients lining the hallways, immobile in their chairs. In the late 1950s and early '60s, nearly six thousand mentally ill persons were crushed into a hospital designed for thousands less. The young job applicants saw an exhausted staff, overworked and undertrained, too harried to respond to all the groans and pleas for help. The scene truly depicted what a Denver newspaper had reproachfully headlined as "city of the damned."

Both saddened by what they saw, and intrigued by the possibilities of how they could help, Gregorio and Haydee Kort returned to their hotel room.

With the trepidation and excitement of two tourists considering their first bungee dive, the two young psychiatrists toted up the risks and rewards of such a harrowing career leap. There were many negatives. Even the new superintendent who interviewed them, Dr. Willis Bower, their prospective boss, warned they might *all* fall on their faces. So they wondered: should they continue their job search or seize the Pueblo opportunity, filled with so many unknowns?

That night they made their fateful decision. Gregorio looked at Haydee and said: "Let's take it and let's see what we can do!"

Over the next twenty-nine years (little did they know), that youthful challenge would turn into the Kort legacy. In 1977, when Haydee became superintendent, their hands were fully untied. Finally, they could complete the revolution in mental health—the process of decentralization—that they had envisioned so many years before through the enlightened eyes of their bosses, Dr. Luis Garcia-Bunuel in Clarinda, Iowa, and Dr. Bower at the Colorado State Hospital in Pueblo.

Once in charge in 1977, the Kort influence began to flow throughout the system like a current of electricity. For Haydee's part, she opened the old hospital system to influential alliances around the state and gave the once beleaguered hospital a new position of authority in the field of mental health. Under her guidance, the hospital forged new professional relationships with the University of Colorado and earned national recognition as a model for decentralized patient care. Her incisive leadership earned her numerous awards, including a national award in 1988 naming her "Most Outstanding Administrator in Mental Health for the Past 25 Years."

Meanwhile, Gregorio was able to fulfill his career goals as a psychiatrist, working closely with patients and staff to probe the causes of individual cases of mental illness and provide customized treatment programs. His innovative ideas to improve the lives of both patients *and* staff were recognized with many awards, including the Distinguished Service Award from the State of Colorado, and a surprise tenth anniversary award that honored him for his "Dedication and Commitment to Staff Development and Quality Patient Care."

Together, the Korts' invigorating presence became so much a part of the ethos and air of the busy daily life of the hospital that staff and patients alike began to refer to their bosses simply as "Dr. H. and Dr. G.," names that were spoken with all the familiarity, affection and confidence of an extended family.

In fact, in some cases, they *were* literally family. The Kort kids, Marcelo and Gabi, became familiar figures at the hospital. They often accompanied their parents to the administration building, where they stayed under the fond and watchful eyes of the clerical staff when Haydee and Gregorio were called away.

Gabi was still very little, but Marcelo was at an age to take part in one of his father's most unique and innovative ideas: to give patients outdoor adventures away from the hospital. Ski trips, camping, football games—Gregorio designed trips that took patients across Colorado. They always included psych techs and professional staff, and often included another psychologist and his son.

"Marcelo would invite his friends too," Gregorio said, "and they all got a good education on what the patients were like. We never had a problem with a patient, and we always had staff along who worked with patients every day and knew how to calm them down. Yes, of course I made sure of Marcelo's safety, but what he gained in experience was well worth it."

Skiing at Monarch Pass; football games at the Air Force Academy; camping in the San Isabel mountain range. Laughing,

Gregorio added, "Some of the patients were more skilled at camping than the staff, and they were able to teach everyone else about camping! That was incredibly rewarding for the patients."

He added, "We did everything we could to offer patients an environment that raised their self-esteem, so when they went back into the community they could say what a good experience it was at the state hospital."

Of course, discomfort often goes hand in hand with innovation. Gregorio said the first time he announced he was taking patients on a ski trip, the reaction of friends and colleagues was, "Well, there goes the community!" But as far as patients were concerned, despite the risks, the new experiences paid off: "Patients would say, 'Well, I have something to tell my friends. Yes, I have been in "the crazy house," but they gave me new adventures. And while I was there I got hearing aids, and they operated on my hernia...' All these positive experiences have an impact."

Encouraged by the results, Gregorio kept adding to the esteem-building experiences.

"We were on a roll," he said with a grin.

"And I wasn't about to stop him," Haydee added, smiling too.

~

One of Gregorio's most rewarding ideas also attracted widespread admiration and acclaim both in Colorado and around the country: the establishment of an art gallery in the patient wings. It earned the Korts one of their numerous awards, invigorated patients and staff, and brought welcome publicity for the hospital.

"We decided that to improve the environment for the patients we would create mini art galleries on each of the two wings," Gregorio recalled. His brainstorming idea was prompted by a magazine cover of the American Psychiatric Association, which had recently featured artwork on its cover as part of a story on the positive impact of artwork and artistic expression in the lives of mentally ill persons.

Gregorio called New York, tracked down the art consultant featured in the article and persuaded her to oversee the establishment of the art gallery. She agreed, not only making a list of famous American Impressionist paintings, but assisting in getting them meticulously reproduced on fine canvas. Soon they were ready to be displayed in the patient wards of the state hospital.

A small flurry of objections arose. Gregorio said, "The naysayers objected, 'It's no use—the patients are going to destroy the paintings in no time. This will have no impact.'" Instead, the patients were the first to embrace the idea. "They were so protective, that when another patient *did* try to do something to the paintings they were the ones who stopped him!"

There was a surprise benefit too: the positive effect on staff and even the surrounding community of Pueblo. "We were so obsessed with doing something for the patients that we didn't realize we had made the staff proud too," Gregorio said. "The paintings had an incredible impact on them; they would even bring their families to see the art gallery on the ward where they worked. Then the local college started to bring art classes to the hospital for tours. That was pretty unique. Everyone was touched, including myself and Haydee."

Staff morale got another boost through Gregorio's idea to introduce family and couples therapy as another treatment option for patients. Family dynamics always play a big a role in a patient's mental health.

But before his staff and psychiatric teams could work effectively in family and couples therapy, Gregorio reasoned, they should know what it was like, so he offered staff members the opportunity to participate first in private therapy sessions with their *own* spouses and family.

If staff felt any early trepidation about opening up their private lives, it evaporated fast. Gregorio smiled, remembering how many staff came up to him after their private sessions to say, "Thank you for what you have done to help my marriage!"

The staff therapy sessions yielded other surprising and unexpected benefits. From staff feedback, Dr. G. learned that successful therapy must take into account culturally sensitive issues. "We learned that if you want to have successful group therapy, don't mix the sexes. For example, no self-respecting Hispanic guy would talk about his problems in front of women," Gregorio said. "It's so simple, but the staff knew this because they were bicultural and bilingual themselves. Likewise, the women wouldn't open up in mixed therapy sessions about themselves or their health. What the staff recommended was, don't refer to the sessions with women as 'psychiatric treatment.' Instead, give the sessions a name, 'Our Bodies, Our Life.' We did that, and in no time the women were opening up and talking about their problems."

～

In her thirteen years as superintendent, Dr. Haydee Kort forged a fresh path for professional women, especially in the field of medicine and psychiatry. But her impact went beyond her gender. Under her leadership the hospital won recognition from many quarters, and even an award as "best psychiatric hospital in the country" by consumer advocate Ralph Nader's organization, which evaluated data from the Accreditation of Health Care Organizations. Haydee received a congratulatory phone call from Colorado Governor Roy Romer, but as she accepted the honor, she gave credit to the hospital's staff and their "day by day dedication."

In one award ceremony the introductory speaker noted, "All during her professional career, her philosophical emphasis has been to help to have the value of the ward-level employees recognized and try to improve their status."

Indeed, both Dr. H. and Dr. G. understood that staff dedication was linked to staff morale and productivity. Early on, they recognized, along with Dr. Bower, that the old "worker drone" system didn't work. Staff were overseeing patients without adequate training and were forced to add janitorial duties to the daily grind. They were overworked, and little more than guards.

That led to the category of specially trained psychiatric technicians. During Haydee's superintendency, other new roles were implemented too. With further education, psych techs could become qualified in the category called "mental health workers," which gave them even more latitude in working with patients.

A nationwide nursing shortage in the 1970s opened the way for another staff innovation. A plan was created to allow the psych techs who wished to become psychiatric nurses to enroll in school at full pay but half their work schedule. In exchange, the new nurses pledged to give the hospital two years of work after they completed their training. The concept seemed radically generous, but it began to return even unexpected dividends.

First of all, "We were assured of a stable, adequate number of trained RNs, and that also assured a big rating for the hospital when the accreditation people came by," Gregorio explained.

There was even a boost to staff morale among those who were *not* interested in joining the new RN program themselves. Gregorio continued: "Even the psych techs that didn't want to continue with nurse's training were very positive about the outcome, because when the former psych techs came back as nurses in a supervisory role, they already understood everything about the psych techs' job—they knew what the psych techs' challenges were. They could say to the psych techs, 'We understand, we have been there.'"

It was one more proof to the Korts that a well-structured staff was a motivated staff. They realized that an overworked staff stirred discontent, and that was true at every employee level, from physicians to groundskeepers.

That truth became personal for Haydee during a round of state-mandated budget trimming. Word had come from on high (via Haydee's boss at the Colorado Division of Mental Health) that three dietary positions would have to be cut. The decision, made administratively miles away "in Denver," would be devastating to the hospital, Haydee knew. Food menus, nutrition planning, and all the elements of kitchen organization flowed from those positions. You might as well imagine whipping together a Thanksgiving dinner feast for a family of twenty, with only one cook allowed in the kitchen!

Haydee, realizing that the proposed cuts spelled kitchen chaos, took a stand.

"But we can't do without those positions!" Haydee protested to Dr. Robert Glover, the director of the Division of Mental Health, who succeeded Dr. Dolby. She had a good relationship with Dr. Glover and that gave her the confidence to push back.

"Come on now, three positions? That's not going to hurt you!" Haydee recalled him saying. Haydee wouldn't back down, so next thing she knew Dr. Glover's boss, Dr. Frank Traylor, the Director of Institutions, was on the phone to say he wanted to meet with the feisty superintendent and find out why she wasn't just doing what she was told.

Haydee and Dr. Traylor had a good relationship too, so she smiled as she recalled their friends-in-combat confrontation:

"Dr. Traylor said, 'Haydee, I'm coming to Pueblo and you're going to explain to me why you can't get rid of three positions, because three positions is *nothing!*' So I lined up the whole dietary group to tell me what those three positions were about: What were their duties? What would happen if they weren't there? My questions went on and on, it was a very good give and take. And about a week later Dr. Traylor comes for his visit.

"He says, 'Listen, Haydee, I don't want to argue, I want you to get rid of those positions.' And I said, 'Dr. Traylor, I want you to listen to why I *cannot.*'

"So I explained to him the whole thing. By that time, I was so into dietary knowledge that you wouldn't believe it. All of a sudden I was like an expert! When I got through with my answer, Dr. Traylor looks at me and says, 'If you want to put that much work in keeping three positions, you *deserve* to keep them. So keep them— and leave me alone!'"

In other ways too, Haydee was willing to shake things up and rattle cages in Denver. From the start of her superintendency, the youthful, first-time superintendent (she was 41 when she took the reins) believed the hospital deserved to be elevated beyond its parochial, small-town status. Both she and Gregorio envisioned opportunities to expand the role of Colorado State Hospital, to make it a motivating authority and advocate for mental health issues throughout the state. To do that they needed the clout and backing of influential leaders in mental health issues, and they had it.

Haydee was already admired for her brief interim leadership at the hospital in Fort Logan; indeed, the folks at the Division of Mental Health clamored for her to take the Fort Logan position permanently, and she had turned it down. A little later, her candidacy for the superintendent job at Pueblo was also supported enthusiastically by Colorado's medical and psychiatric community.

The bottom line was, she knew she could count on them for long-term support: "I didn't have any qualms asking for their help."

And so, early in her superintendency, with much goodwill capital to spare, Dr. H. turned her networking skills to a major project. Her goal was to transform the Colorado State Hospital in Pueblo from an "also-ran" in the eyes of the medical and educational establishments into a respected teaching institution in the field of mental health. Somehow, living in Pueblo and practicing psychiatry at the State Hospital *had* to be transformed into an attractive career destination.

To do that, Haydee reached out to the state's most influential institution in the field of medicine and psychiatry, the University of Colorado.

Up to then, the hospital faced a big image problem: young doctors simply weren't interested in leaving Denver to work in small-town Pueblo. So Haydee turned to Dr. James Shore, chairman of the University of Colorado's Department of Psychiatry. "I wanted to create a liaison with the university, because it represented the most powerful group of psychiatrists in the state," Haydee explained.

Together, Haydee and Dr. Shore created a new position, Director of Education at the Colorado State Hospital in Pueblo. The first appointment was Dr. Jay Scully from the University of Colorado. Under his leadership, the hospital forged a strong liaison with the university, and young psychiatric residents began to view the once gloomy and stultified state hospital as an intriguing next step in their careers. Until then, most young residents couldn't be pried away from Denver. After all, to be in Colorado's largest city, with all its amenities and urban attractions, surely was the more attractive place to work and live; besides, the pay was far better!

Haydee and Dr. Shore solved the pay problem too. They hammered out an arrangement with the University of Colorado, which agreed to fill in the salary gap by paying psychiatry residents working in Pueblo through the university system. That made the residents' pay in Pueblo competitive with Denver.

Did it work? The answer came quickly. Soon six to eight young psychiatrists had moved to Pueblo for the career residency program. "We were delighted," Haydee said. "Recruitment had been so difficult until then, and to have these career residents was wonderful."

Once in Pueblo, career residents received incomparable, personalized clinical experience and instruction. As Director of Adult Psychiatric Services, Dr. G. opened their eyes to the relatively new fields of family and couples therapy, and the benefits and challenges of placing qualified mentally ill persons back in their hometowns and communities.

"To combine good clinical experience and instruction was to give them the best possible rotation," Gregorio said. "I would see residents once a week, where I would give them a sounding board to discuss cases, shoot the breeze, and examine different therapies. It was a time to round out their experience, a time to prove themselves and decide a career track."

Under Gregorio's personalized direction, young physicians had direct access to cutting-edge ideas and innovations in patient care. "It was clear to us that we could offer a very complete program, the fullest spectrum of clinical experience and instruction," Gregorio said.

On the recommendation of Dr. Shore, Gregorio was nominated for, and received, The Nancy Roeske Recognition Award of the American Psychiatric Association for his work in pioneering the education program at the Colorado State Hospital. Dr. Shore cited Gregorio as being "instrumental in the development of the first psychiatry educational program for medical students from the University of Colorado outside the Denver urban area," and for "changing the attitudes of future Colorado physicians" toward the mentally ill. In his recommendation letter, Dr. Shore noted the high regard students had for Dr. G. and wrote, "They mentioned him as a warm, charismatic, funny teacher who related well to patients and was a wonderful role model for them in dealing with very sick patients and their families."

Once the program was underway, it exceeded everyone's expectations.

"Everything like this helped," Gregorio agreed. "To have a

relationship with the Department of Psychiatry at the University of Colorado improved the prestige of the hospital."

As for the experience of the residents? Gregorio paused and smiled.

"The student feedback was so positive that everybody was lining up to come to the state hospital!"

~

Building a relationship with the University of Colorado proved to be a winning strategy for the State Hospital in Pueblo. Haydee had seen to it that the university connection attracted medical and psychiatric talent to Pueblo (and provided comparable salaries), and now she saw a wider application.

Fresh in the hospital's collective memory was a bitter 1974 labor dispute over inadequate pay for nurses in the maximum-security unit, and a potentially dangerous lack of security in the unit as well. The dispute erupted into a nine-day strike in July 1974. While the swift resolution between the hospital and AFCSME Local 123 was considered a landmark success story in Colorado labor relations, there was no salary relief.

Three years later, Haydee, now the superintendent, was keenly aware of the nagging and unresolved salary issues at the hospital. The University of Colorado had closed the gap in pay for its young physicians who came to work in Pueblo. If the state hospital in Pueblo was competitive salary-wise with Denver and other comparable hospitals around the country, that would elevate Pueblo as a teaching institution.

The idea, propelled forward by Haydee's enthusiasm and

backed by Dr. Shore at the University of Colorado, won the support of the Colorado State Board of Mental Health. Before long, all hospital physicians became salaried employees of the University of Colorado system.

The arrangement was believed to be unique, nationwide. "It's an example of what you can accomplish when everyone works together," Gregorio said.

The working relationship between Haydee and Dr. Shore at the University of Colorado became an enduring and trusting one, so much so that they worked in tandem even on sensitive personnel issues.

One time a young doctor was assigned to work in Pueblo. However, the newcomer proved to be an uncomfortable fit. He didn't get along with staff or work effectively with patients. Dr. Shore, who had a supervisory role over the young man, called Haydee and posed the question: "If he was on *your* staff, what would you do?"

"I would fire him," Haydee said promptly.

"So Dr. Shore did," Haydee recalled. "I couldn't believe he would take my word for it just like that—but he did. He fired him."

Measure by measure, year by year, the reputation and buzz grew louder, that the once old, decrepit and "damned" Colorado State Hospital was alive with fresh ideas, some new, and some updated to suit the times. Slowly but surely, the old hospital was becoming a potent force in the field of mental health:

— A Hispanic Treatment Program was established in the Adult

Psychiatric Service thanks to a $300,000 grant from the National Institute of Health. The program, ahead of its time in recognizing the needs of non-English-speaking patients, called for wards staffed completely by bilingual and bicultural staff. The program won a Certificate of Achievement Award from the American Psychiatric Association in 1981.

— Programs that targeted specific mental health problems and demographic groups flourished during the Kort years. They included a Geriatric Treatment Center, as well as a program for mentally ill children to be treated along with their families, and a program for mentally ill persons with drug abuse complications.

— The hospital, once a forbidding place whose image was the threat, "Behave or we'll take you to 13th Street!" opened itself to the world in 1979 for Colorado's Centennial celebration. The three-day public event, "100 Years of Caring" featured a concert by Air Force personnel, an antique car parade, a barbecue and the burial of a time capsule, to be opened in 2079. It was a far cry from the walled-off, prison-like setting that defined the founding of the hospital a century before.

As always, the Korts kept focused on the idea that took root at the core and beginning of their professional careers, that *decentralization* was best for patients as well as society at large. By the end of their tenure in 1990, the Korts' commitment to decentralization had reduced the population from an unmanageable six thousand patients to six hundred.

In the spirit of decentralization, Gregorio realized that it created a more efficient system if potential patients were evaluated *first* in their own local community mental health centers, *before* coming to the state hospital.

"We were clear in our minds that the success of our philosophy was to have the evaluations start at the mental health centers in the community," Gregorio explained. "Did the patient really need to be admitted? So we told them, 'We want them to be evaluated in your local community first, and then we will take your recommendation.'"

Thanks to the Korts' commitment to decentralization, by the time Drs. H. and G. retired, they had each been recognized numerous times for their groundbreaking work, and as a news story in the *Pueblo Chieftain* noted in 1990, "Institutions across the country model their treatment programs around those at (the Colorado State Hospital)."

As late as 2017, a full twenty-seven years after her retirement, an editorial in the *Pueblo Chieftain* called Haydee "a tireless advocate" and noted that "the state hospital once thrived under (her) leadership."

No one program or idea propelled the decentralization of Colorado State Hospital and made it the pacesetter in the understanding and care of the mentally ill. Over their thirty years at the hospital, Gregorio and Haydee built on one idea after another, seizing opportunities as they arose, always rising to the challenge they'd posed to each other so many years before: "Let's see what we can do!"

CHAPTER FOURTEEN

MIXED FEELINGS, MANY MEMORIES

On a sunny July day in 1990, Gregorio and Haydee Kort drove their usual two-mile route to the Colorado State Hospital, well aware this was not just another day.

Just the month before, on June 6, 1990, they had officially retired, and on this July day they were coming back for a big party in their honor. The celebration was scheduled for the day after Independence Day, a fitting high-water mark for the Korts' thirty years of groundbreaking service to Colorado State Hospital. In 1990 the name was changed to CMHIP, the Colorado Mental Health Institute in Pueblo.

For several months, the Korts had been treated to a round of farewell rituals and celebrations befitting their standing in Pueblo and in Colorado. They arrived in 1961 to practice psychiatry and help the mentally ill, and in the process, by their retirement in 1990 they had achieved something of legendary status at the hospital, in the state of Colorado, and even around the country. Other state hospitals emulated their policies.

At their retirement, praise for the Korts poured in from all over the state and country, from the Pueblo City Council to the governor of Colorado. The city council honored Haydee by declaring "Haydee Kort Day," in honor of the first woman superintendent of a state hospital. She was honored nationally as the "Outstanding Administrator in Mental Health for the Past 25 Years" and given a special award as President of the American Association of Psychiatric Administrators. Even in a wave of awards, that one was special, Haydee said, "and it took me completely by surprise."

Together, the couple had gathered in many honors over the years, and Gregorio had his own moment of surprise when he received a special and unexpected anniversary award from his colleagues for his years of clinical work with patients and as Director of the Adult Psychiatric Services Division.

As for the official retirement party, that was set in motion by Nell Mitchell, who along with her husband Bob had something special in mind. Nell, the longtime hospital historian and museum director, and her husband Bob, who passed away in 2018, had been working on the project for countless months along with the appreciative hospital staff. They had even secretly gathered information from the Korts' families in Argentina.

Nell's surprise would come at the very end as the capstone of the July celebration, and like everything else that day, it was a labor of love.

Love for the Korts came easy to Nell and Bob Mitchell. Nell joined the hospital in 1962 as a young administrative assistant, just a year after Gregorio and Haydee came to Pueblo. She saw their impact on the hospital through the years.

Today, from the vantage point of 2018, Nell says, "Thank God she was superintendent! She really knew how to run the place. She knew what needed to be done, and that's why she went into administration, to have more of an impact. She really helped the hospital and improved it in so many ways. I think she was the best superintendent we ever had."

Nell arrived the year after the two young psychiatrists arrived for their milestone-making job interview. From their nondescript hotel room, Gregorio and Haydee debated whether the jobs offered them by the new superintendent, Dr. Willis Bower, were worth taking. They knew they wanted to work together as psychiatrists, but was this the right place to build their careers? The hospital was gloomy, overcrowded, even menacing, the punchline to a dark joke that parents used with their unruly kids: "You better behave or we'll take you to 13th Street!"

One longtime hospital employee recalled joining the hospital as a teenage volunteer in the 1970s, even before the Korts took charge. "I worked there in high school to build up my college resume," the employee recalled. "When Haydee became superintendent, she changed it from an 'institutional' institution to a place where people actually were able to live."

～

On that July day in 1990, Gregorio and Haydee knew a big party was waiting for them on the lawn and that a crowd of employees, patients and dignitaries would be there. But they didn't know about the parade, and they didn't know about a surprise that was scheduled for the very end, which came about thanks to Nell and Bob Mitchell's work.

Even before all the surprises were unveiled, "That day was something I will never forget," said Gregorio, smiling at the memory.

The first unforgettable surprise was the parade in the open-top convertible. Haydee and Gregorio found themselves on the topmost seat, facing an appreciative and applauding crowd that lined the drive. Along the way they saw so many staff they had worked with over the years, and patients too. Perhaps the sight of the patients was best of all—more than anything else, Haydee and Gregorio's thirty-year mission had been to free individuals from the oppression of mental illness, and allow them the opportunity to live in the world again.

Now so many of those patients, including grateful former patients, were standing there and applauding as the Korts passed by.

One of those patients was "James."

"He was the most gentle person you could think of except when he got drunk and beat his mother up," Gregorio recalled. "And one to one, I would sit him down and chastise him for not having feeling for his mother. 'I understand it's the alcohol talking,' I said, 'but you have to take control before that first shot.' Well, he didn't quit right away, but he was embarrassed and apologetic and sincere. Eventually when his mother got ill, he quit drinking and took care of his mother."

James had turned around his life, and much of his success could be attributed to one of Gregorio's innovative insights: that one's family, friends—"ordinary" people in the community—were as important to a patient's recovery as the professional staff. Gregorio put that idea into play with his outreach to individuals in the community. In the early years of decentralization, he had persuaded a boarding-home owner to switch her business instead to providing a home for patients, and he encouraged the psych technician assigned to the case to document the success in a paper for a psychiatric publication. As Gregorio put it, "We tried to identify those people in the community that may be key to help with the planning of a patient's future."

When James was ready to return to his hometown in the San Luis Valley, Gregorio even envisioned a way to involve the local sheriff in James' recovery.

"The sheriff was very unhappy with the number of times he had to arrest James. He didn't feel that should be his role," Gregorio said. "But he wanted to help."

So Gregorio used his enlistment talents to bring the sheriff on board: "We put him on the planning team for the San Luis Valley Mental Health Center."

When James was ready to leave the hospital, Gregorio enlisted the sheriff in another job. "I talked to him, and as a friendly gesture to us, the sheriff agreed to supervise James, pick him up at the bus station, monitor him, and make sure he was taking his medication for alcoholics."

As it turned out, besides being an excellent law enforcement officer, Sheriff Navarro had some hidden talents. With a grin, Gregorio summed it up: "Besides being a good sheriff, he was a good therapist!"

As for James, he never forgot the help he received from Gregorio, his therapist who set him on the track to sobriety and a stable life. James came to the retirement party, and said something to Gregorio that the doctor never forgot: "Dr. Kort, I poured my soul out to you and now you are leaving me!"

~

At the retirement party, and in the years that have followed, Gregorio and Haydee have had reason to remember many other moments that filled their professional careers.

Gregorio remembered the very earliest years, as far back as Tennessee, when he would listen to the beautiful spirituals sung by his African American patients. As a young psychiatrist, it was one of his first clinical experiences in understanding the value of treating each patient as an individual, a concept he would follow for the rest of his professional career. "I loved to listen to them sing," he said, "it gave me insight into their lives and helped me to understand and find new ways to help them…"

Haydee remembered "Stella," a young woman, only twenty years old, who killed her kids by suffocating them to death with a pillow.

"That one was really, really hard," Haydee said. "She was in the hospital for several years." Stella was diagnosed as a schizophrenic paranoid with severe depression. As with each patient, her treatment was a careful and methodical exercise in finding the right combination of drugs, psychiatric counseling and other therapies, sometimes including electroshock treatments. Slowly, after a series of successes and setbacks, the young woman regained her stability. "She got to the point where she regretted what she did," Haydee said. "She recognized that it was her mistake, and that her illness did not absolve her from culpability—yes, she did it *because* she was very ill, but then she took culpability."

From the most tragic of stories, the happiest and most unexpected of endings: Stella was finally released from the hospital, and she married a fellow patient she met on the ward. Together, the two built a peaceable life and continued their quiet recovery.

Then there was "Mary," who for many years ran a stylish

boutique in another city in Colorado. To her customers she was the shop owner with the ever-gracious smile, impeccably dressed, the kind of "put-together" woman every other woman wanted to emulate.

For a reason no one could understand, not even Mary, the day came when her seemingly disciplined life shattered into chaotic pieces. Who knows how long the crisis was in the making? Whether it was sudden onset or slowly building, one day Mary was overtaken by a severe depression that was as paralyzing as if she had broken her spine. The depression became so profound that she could not leave her home. In despair, her family brought her to the Colorado State Mental Hospital. After an evaluation, Gregorio and Haydee consulted together and decided she might be another good candidate for electroshock treatments.

Controversial then and now, a device often featured in old horror movies, electroconvulsive shock therapy, which dates back to 1937, never completely deserved its negative image, the Korts point out. That's not to say it wasn't used in damaging ways in its early years, but that was because of inexperience with using electricity, inherently dangerous, on living subjects. "When it's used correctly, and with the proper patient, it can be a valuable tool in their recovery," Gregorio said.

To everybody's surprise, Mary turned out to be the ideal electroshock patient. After three short treatments, she was herself again. Fortified by counseling and anti-depression medication, she returned to her hometown and spent years working and living happily.

As far as customers knew, the shop owner with the gracious smile had never left.

~

On the retirement parade day, James was there, and so were other grateful patients like Stella and Mary. They lined the driveway and waved at Gregorio and Haydee as they passed by. A large crowd of hospital staff was there too. Over and over again the convertible slowed to a halt as a patient or staff member stepped out of the crowd to say thank you.

Inch by inch, propelled forward by the appreciative crowd, the convertible made its way from the administration building to a venerable old brick building. The fact it was standing there at all in 1990 was because it owed its continued existence to Haydee's foresight. It happened to be the former superintendent's house.

The last superintendent to live there was Dr. Charles Meredith, who moved out in 1977. The Korts followed right after his tenure, but they chose to raise their kids, Marcelo and Gabi, on a cozy and charming neighborhood street. Unoccupied, the brooding brick mansion quickly become a sulking white elephant. As both Nell Mitchell and Haydee recalled, the facilities manager on the grounds, as well as the top brass in the Division of Mental Health in Denver, were of one mind: "Get rid of it!"

Raze the superintendent's building? No way! "Haydee told them to renovate it," Nell recalled, chuckling. "They didn't want to do it and she said, 'You WILL do it!'"

Haydee saw that it would make a fine museum. And in fact, while it was completely unsuitable as a hospital facility and mournfully inadequate as a family home, the former superintendent's house *was* suitable, amazingly so, as the CMHIP Museum—the historical repository of the Colorado Mental Health Institute Hospital Museum. So it is to this day.

By 1990, the day of the Kort celebration, the museum was already known as the showcase of the hospital's heritage. Renovated, scrubbed and freshened, the exterior was welcoming and the interior rooms offered a naturally graceful progression of artifacts and photos going back to the hospital's opening in 1879.

On tours, visitors can step right up to the old telephone switchboard, a ghostly reminder of the many calls for help that flooded the hospital over the decades. Old electroshock machines, a "restraint chair," and the heavy desk of a long-ago superintendent have their place here. Countless patient artifacts have been preserved, including shaving mugs, tobacco tins and a barber chair. Throughout are historic photos, from official superintendent portraits to the informal snapshots of patients at picnics and football games.

The Korts already knew the museum, of course. Nell and Bob Mitchell and their team had begun filling the museum space in about 1985, but the idea had been growing since the late 1970s. "During the Centennial in 1979, we had found all these artifacts and documents that had been put away and forgotten," Nell said. "These were things about the history of the hospital I never knew existed, and I thought, 'This is something that has to be done.'"

From then on, Nell, Bob and eager volunteers from the hospital staff knew they had a project on their hands. They plunged into all the forgotten nooks and crannies of the hospital: grim attic spaces, musty corners of neglected buildings, ancient file cabinets. Under their inquisitive hands, the historical record began unfolding from the beginning, from the years when it was known by its menacing first name, the Colorado State Insane Asylum, to its rebirth as the Colorado State Hospital, when Haydee and Gregorio Kort elevated its reputation and mission, to its current reconfiguration as the Colorado Mental Health Institute in Pueblo (CMHIP).

On that bittersweet farewell day in 1990, Nell and Bob Mitchell had something fresh and exciting to give the Korts. When the parade and the speeches had ended, Dr. H. and Dr. G. were escorted into the museum and brought to a brand-new room—the Kort Room. The room in the museum is dedicated to the Korts' successes and the tenure of Superintendent Haydee Kort.

Haydee and Gregorio walked into the museum that day unprepared for what they would see. "Haydee was very surprised," Nell Mitchell recalled. "She came over and gave me a big hug, and so did Greg."

To this day, the impact of the Kort Room is as powerful to Haydee and Gregorio as it was the day it was unveiled to them, and it still leaves them short of words. "Oh, it was wonderful," Haydee said. "The day was already everything we could ask for; this was an unexpected bonus," said Gregorio.

To walk into the Kort Room was to be enveloped in a time capsule. Photos, awards and artifacts of their tenure filled the walls. For weeks Nell Mitchell, her husband Bob, and their hospital team had secretly gathered up Kort-era photos, documents, even background material from their youthful days in Argentina.

"I decided that because of all the things they had done for the hospital, the patients and staff, that when they retired they deserved this tribute," Nell said. "It was a retirement present from me and Bob."

Nearly thirty years later, in 2017, Nell set out to grow the Kort Room with even more material, but this time she went right to

Haydee and Gregorio to ask what they wanted to include. The Internet era had given the Mitchells more tools to work with. "With all the new media possibilities now, it's not cut and paste anymore," Nell said. "I'd give the pictures and captions and comments to the media guy, and told him where I wanted them to be spaced. He runs it through the computer and shows it to me on a big TV screen and says, 'Is this the way you want it?'"

"I just wanted to make it look better and make it totally their room," Nell said. "It was important to me that the first woman superintendent of the hospital have a room dedicated to her tenure."

In the years since their retirement, Gregorio and Haydee have hardly been quiet; their active lives simply veered down other avenues. First and foremost has been enjoying their children, Marcelo and Gabi, and four treasured grandchildren, Stephanie, Andrew, Natalia and Sofia, and a growing brood of grandchildren. There have been countless trips to Argentina and points around the world, including South America, Europe and Japan.

As for the town of Pueblo, in 1961 it looked like a doubtful place to spend a lifetime, but it has become the Korts' beloved hometown. Their daughter Gabi jokes that she tried to lure them to relocate to be nearer to her in Arizona, but they would have none of it! Pueblo is their home. Fast friendships bind them too, and with their cherished friends the Korts travel, attend the opera and symphony concerts, and enjoy collecting artwork.

Yet their years at the Colorado State Hospital continue to follow them, not just in memory but in legacy. Gregorio's creative and groundbreaking efforts to motivate patients with the joy and beauty of life, by involving them with art, sports and activities, is considered groundbreaking work in the field of mental illness.

As for Haydee, the struggles she engaged in with policymakers and the press as superintendent have long since given way to their admiration for her.

As late as 2017, a full twenty-seven years after her retirement, the *Pueblo Chieftain* cited Haydee in an editorial, praising her as a tireless advocate for the mentally ill. In one simple sentence, the newspaper summed up an era when two youthful psychiatrists came to Colorado and showed the state, and later the nation, that there was a better way to treat mental illness. It concluded: "The state hospital once thrived under the leadership of former Superintendent Dr. Haydee Kort."

CHAPTER FIFTEEN

FAMILY FIRST

During the day, Dr. Haydee Kort headed the entire Colorado State Hospital system as Superintendent, while Dr. Gregorio Kort managed the hospital's clinical side as Director of Adult Psychiatric Services. But in the evening, a new boss took over: family. From their youngest days as parents Haydee and Gregorio lived by the rule "Home by Five," and their beloved two children came first. Their son and daughter, Marcelo and Gabriela (Gabi), share their insights about growing up with two parents who happened to be psychiatrists—but first and foremost, they were Mom and Dad.

Marcelo Kort

Marcelo Kort was born May 12, 1959 in Memphis, Tennessee. He served in the office of State Planning and Budget for Governor Roy Romer from 1989 to 1998. He currently works for Eli Lilly and Company in government affairs. He and his wife Allison live in Littleton, Colorado. They have given Gregorio and Haydee two beloved grandchildren, Stephanie and Andrew.

It's always been interesting having two parents as psychiatrists; my sister and I couldn't have asked for two better people. I think because of their background they have always been more in tune with their children than many parents are. When we were kids they were not only aware of what we were doing, but they were always asking, "How is your day? How are things going?"

I remember whenever issues came up—all the ups and downs of childhood—they were always so great at being able to help. They picked up when I was preoccupied with something, when something was going on with friends or something didn't go well on a test. They were always asking, "Do you want to talk about it?"

They wanted us to know, "We're always here for you."

Now that I'm a parent I know this from experience: You try to raise your kids well, and hope you've done a good job, and one of the ways you can tell is whether in times of crisis or adversity or when you need someone, do you turn to your parents first? In our case the answer was always yes. Sure, you get scared as a kid over something you did—"Oh, Mom and Dad are gonna kill me!"—but Gabi and I were never scared to come to our parents for anything, no matter what we did. We never hesitated because we knew they would understand.

Probably one of the reasons their marriage is so successful is because they have such complementary personalities. My father is a fly by the seat of the pants, roll with the punches kind of person, while my mother is very much a person who is in charge, and must know all the details.

My mother enjoyed the challenge of being superintendent and dealing with the political and public sides of things, while my father was much more comfortable staying clinically focused on patients.

When they came home at the end of the day they would spend a lot of time talking about things going on at the hospital, and my mother would bounce things off of my father. She trusted him completely, and he trusted her. They always shared their insights with each other.

My parents wanted to make sure we understood what mental health was all about. When we were kids they took us to the hospital, where we'd sit with the administrative staff while they worked, and when we got home they'd ask, "Is there anything you saw today that you want to talk about? Anything you want to ask?" Some patients may have been experiencing very psychotic symptoms and they might end up doing strange things, and my parents always wanted to make sure we understood *why*. They wanted us to know, "Mental illness is something that can touch anybody. These individuals have brain disorders that any of us could have." Gabi and I grew up understanding this, and this was a blueprint for us in understanding, and eliminating, the stigma and fear of mental illness. So I appreciate that my parents helped me with that at such a young age. It helped me in my future relationships and in my work.

Certainly, years later, this was very important in my work in government affairs with Eli Lilly. One of the reasons I jumped at the job opportunity was because when I joined the company, we were doing a lot of things in the field of neuroscience, and the company was heavily involved in bringing medications for the treatment of mental illness to market, such as Prozac. So of course, it was valuable experience to have two parents as psychiatrists, and to have the experience of spending time at the hospital with patients. It was like having my personal and professional life come full circle. Even after they retired I kept my parents involved, and arranged to have them come to company events to give talks on mental health treatments and medications.

You asked about what it was like to spend time with the patients at the hospital. I remember my dad arranged so many activities for patients and staff, and I joined in too. There was a swimming pool at the hospital, and softball games, camping, skiing, football games at the Air Force Academy...we did many things together.

I remember one time when we went camping, we were putting up tents and deciding where to sleep, and Dad called me over and said, "We're going to be sleeping near some patients and staff—if you're worried about that, let me know." I told him, "No, I'm not worried at all." And my dad looked at me and said, "That's good, you should be less worried about the patients than about sleeping next to me, because of the way I snore!"

That's typical of my dad. He's very humorous, always kidding, and it's hard to get him to stay serious about anything. The fact my father is so laid back and my mother is more serious and straightforward, I think that's why they have been so successful in their marriage and professional lives.

This will give you an idea of how different they were. I remember one time—this was while my mother was superintendent—there was a very important hospital accreditation meeting at the hospital that involved the governor, the director of the division of mental health, a large group of mental health dignitaries, all the top brass in the state. It was a very stiff and formal meeting. And they all were going around the table introducing themselves.

Finally, they get to my father. And he says in a very solemn way,

"I am Dr. Gregorio Kort, Director of Adult Psychiatric Services at Colorado State Hospital, and if you wonder how I kept my job all these years, I sleep with the superintendent!"

Well, everybody cracked up. It was wonderful. But my mother was mortified. She told people later that she wanted to crawl under the table. "How could you do that, in *that* setting?" My father said, "You should thank me! The meeting turned out to be successful and it wasn't so stiff." He knew if she took things too intensely, he could bring her around with his humor. She can never be mad at my dad for long.

They may be very different in their personalities, but their values are in complete harmony. The most important thing they've taught me is to treat everyone with respect and dignity. They taught me the value of hearing other people out, listening to what they have to say, and taking time to understand what they are going through. They taught me to be *there* for people. And don't ever become too opinionated about things, because nobody's perfect.

I couldn't have been blessed by better parents.

～

Gabi Kort Iturri

Gabriela (Gabi) Kort Iturri was born December 13, 1963 in Pueblo, Colorado. She worked in human resources management in the hospitality industry and as a licensed insurance broker, and currently is a mentor volunteer at a boys' and girls' club for underprivileged children. She and her husband Joe live in Scottsdale, Arizona. They have given Gregorio and Haydee two beloved granddaughters, Natalia and Sofia.

My parents are both warm and welcoming to everyone, whether that person is a president of a company or a homeless person on the street. They taught me never to believe I was above someone else, and I think I got that quality from them, that everyone deserves the same treatment.

My memories of growing up in Pueblo are good. I lived there until I was 18 years old and made lifelong friends there, before leaving to go to the University of Colorado in Boulder. Looking back, I didn't realize how lucky I was to have two psychiatrists as parents; it was definitely a plus, and some of my friends would come to them for advice. When I met my husband, Joe, he told his friends, "My girlfriend's parents are both psychiatrists. Do you think they're going to try to analyze me?" Of course they made him feel comfortable right away, and he adores them.

My mom and dad are both great parents, but they have very different personalities. Dad is a sweetheart, with a great sense of humor. He's more easygoing; he doesn't like conflict. Mom is competitive. She's more of a take-charge person, but she is the first to say she would never have been superintendent without Dad behind her. She's always turned to him for advice.

I was born on Friday the thirteenth—that's not considered anything in Argentina and my parents aren't superstitious—but it was 11:55 p.m. on the thirteenth and so the doctor asks my mother, "Do you want to wait five minutes for the birth?" and my mother says, "Absolutely not!" That's my mom's personality, straightforward and no-nonsense.

Here's a story about my dad. I've played tennis most of my life, on varsity high school teams, at state tournaments and currently play on two women's leagues. Anyway, when I was in middle school I went to the country club to take lessons with my dad. He had played tennis and I hadn't. The coach knew both of us. At a certain point in my training the coach goes over to my dad and says: "It's totally switched; she's better than you now!" My dad just laughed it off, he was proud of me.

My mother on the other hand is very competitive. I remember making the number-one spot on the high school varsity tennis team, but the coach took me aside and thought I should play the number-two spot, because the match-up better suited my strengths and the type of game I played.

My mother completely objected to that: "You earned the number-one spot and you should play the number-one spot!" That's how competitive my mom is. For me the right thing was to take my coach's advice. As it turned out, playing the number-two spot was the right thing to do.

While they have very different personalities, they have both always been there for me. Even though my mother was a very intense person as superintendent, whenever I'd call her at work she would drop everything to take my call. When I went to college in Boulder, I found it a big adjustment and I struggled at times. But I knew I could call my parents ten times a day if needed and they would always be there to listen. They always were there for me.

We were so lucky, Marcelo and I, to be able to travel extensively as we were growing up. Because we had relatives in Argentina, we would go there every two or three years, and we went to Central America, Japan, Hawaii, the Bahamas, and Mexico. Later, I was able to study abroad in southern Spain, and my parents came to visit me there.

My husband Joe—or Jose, as we also call him—is a

first-generation American, like I am. His family is from Spain and of course mine is from Argentina. I met him when we were both in the hotel business and living in San Diego. Yes, to answer your question, I think the fact I married a person who came from another country, as my parents did, was probably a factor in our getting together; his family comes from a different background than mine, but he has that same culturally Hispanic warmth as my parents do.

I think growing up with psychiatrists as parents gave us a great advantage. It's not that Marcelo and I can "read into people" like they can, but we definitely have a sensitivity towards others, and an ability to listen to people's stories, and I think we get that from our parents.

They give everyone a chance. Here's how accepting they are. Melba Stockwell was our nanny, and she cared for us kids from the time when we were little. Melba came from a poor family, and she didn't drive. So Dad would pick her up every morning, and every night after he got home from work he would turn right around and drive her home. Melba was very religious too, and I remember both my mom and dad were so accepting of her faith. All they asked of her was, "Just take good care of our kids!"

There are so many amazing stories I can share about my parents. They just adore our kids; when Natalia and Sofia were little they flew to our home in Arizona so my husband and I could take advantage of travel opportunities. They have always been kind to those outside our family too. When I was in college, I had a friend whose parents got divorced, and her mother had a hard time finding a job, so my mother got her a job at the state hospital.

If you ask anyone in Pueblo, anyone who knows them, they will tell you the same thing: My parents weren't only successful in their professional lives, but to this day they are kind and sensitive to everyone they meet.

CHAPTER SIXTEEN

OTHER VOICES

Through the years, both at the Colorado State Hospital and in their personal lives, Dr. H. and Dr. G. forged strong loyalties with colleagues and made many friends. Often, colleagues became friends. These are memories from a few of the many people whose lives were touched by Gregorio and Haydee Kort.

~

Dr. Jay Scully

Dr. James (Jay) Scully enrolled in the University of Colorado psychiatric residency program in 1973 after leaving the Navy. In the late 1970s he was named Director of Medical Student Education in the Department of Psychiatry at the University of Colorado, and began working collaboratively with Superintendent Dr. Haydee Kort and Clinical Director Dr. Gregorio Kort to develop a Career Residency program with the Colorado State Hospital and the University of Colorado Medical School Department of Psychiatry. He later became vice chairman of the Department of Psychiatry and was in charge of all medical education programs for the university. In 1992 Dr. Scully became Director of the Office of Education and Deputy Medical

Director for the American Psychiatric Association. He later held key positions at the University of South Carolina, including Chair of Neuropsychiatry, before returning to the American Psychiatric Association as Medical Director and CEO until his retirement in 2014.

We were looking for a place outside of the city to place medical students, and Haydee was interested. My agenda was to get students out of Denver and into rural communities and outside of the Medical Center—I had a federal grant to do that—and I wasn't getting anywhere. Somebody said, "How about the state hospital in Pueblo?" and I thought, "OK, I think this can work."

So we worked out a placement program with the students and it turned out to be a very popular rotation. They were treated very well and learned a great deal at the state hospital.

So for years, every week on Thursdays, I would drive down to Pueblo and spend the day there to see the students and to do consultations with interesting cases.

In my career I've always tended to get promoted into administrative positions, and I suppose because of that I've always been interested in how people administer things. And as an administrator, Haydee was a fireball! Very impressive. In my life I've had the good fortune to have some outstanding mentors and administrators to look up to, and Haydee was one of them.

I will always remember her style. It was exceptionally effective but different than those I had seen up to that time; it was a feminine, almost a maternal style, rather than hierarchal like a man's. In other words, she was clearly in charge but in a subtle way. If she got pushed, well that was it, she had no problem saying, "I'm in charge," but first, she tried to get people to get along and to understand the situation. That was her first solution. She knew how to be total iron, totally strong, but she didn't push it on anybody.

I remember one episode. I was in Pueblo, and a couple of the ward chiefs were fighting with one another. We all knew each other, and each of these ward chiefs wanted me to take his side in the dispute. I said to Haydee, "What are you going to do about this?" and she said, "I'm not going to do anything. They have to work this out themselves." In other words, she treated them like adults, not like boys fighting in a schoolyard.

But my reaction was, "They'll never learn," and then I watched the outcome, and I had to say, "My goodness, that worked!" I think that was something a woman would do. Rather than impose her will on them, Haydee stayed very much in charge but she did it in an effective and subtle kind of way. She was one of the best administrators I have ever seen.

I loved Greg. He was a superb clinician who knew how to take care of very problematic patients. He was very good at what he did. I don't think you could get that quality of care in Denver. I remember driving down to Pueblo with other medical staff from the university, various people who wanted to observe how things were being handled at the state hospital, and on the way back we'd remark, "Wow, patients are being really taken care of in Pueblo. The people in Denver need to know that."

Greg was gentle but strong, if you know what I mean, and he was very comfortable taking care of very sick people, and being clinical chief. Of course, he also has a wicked sense of humor, a very dry sense of humor, and he was not diminished at all by the fact that Haydee did all the budgeting and politics and all the stuff that was necessary to do administratively.

Haydee was very good dealing with politics and press. Once, while she was superintendent, they had an incident where a pregnant patient had to be put into restraints, and it became public. It just so happened that the press showed up with a photographer and somehow a photograph was taken of the patient in restraints. Now, you'd think that was something a superintendent would never want to have happen, except the next thing you know, Haydee got the financial resources from the state to make sure that kind of a situation never happened again.

So she got what she wanted. The fact the press was there for that incident was probably because Haydee called them! She was always fighting for resources and for her folks and for patients.

There are three programs in the country that were seen as innovative state models for mental health. They were in Maryland, in Oregon—and in Pueblo, Colorado. That never would have happened without Haydee and Greg.

I also want to say Haydee and Greg have done a remarkably positive thing for immigrants. We are a country of immigrants—in fact, I'm a first-generation American, my father was born in Ireland—and Haydee and Greg are examples of the great contributions that immigrants make to our country and culture. Today, more than ever, we need to be reminded of that.

∾

Dr. Elissa Ball and Dr. Jay Richter
Dr. Elissa Ball and Dr. Jay Richter were young married physicians when they were coaxed from Denver to Pueblo in 1985 by Colorado State Hospital Superintendent Dr. Haydee Kort.

Dr. Ball joined the hospital as a psychiatry resident and later was named as the hospital's Chief of Psychiatry. Today she is a retired forensic psychiatrist working as a patient advocate in Pueblo. She also volunteers at The Friendly Harbor, a community drop-in center for individuals and their families who are coping with mental health and substance conditions.

Dr. Richter joined the Colorado State Hospital as a physician specializing in internal medicine, and was Chief of the Department of Medicine from 1987 to 1994. Today he is a retired internist.

The couple have lived in Pueblo for more than thirty years.

$\sim$

DR. ELISSA BALL: We first met Haydee and Greg Kort in 1985 when we started making plans to take jobs at the Colorado State Hospital. Pretty quickly we were able to negotiate a plan to have our medical insurance covered while we went on a trip to New Zealand. It was more than that they were accommodating; they were very, very invested in getting good psychiatrists and good internists to stay with the hospital.

Haydee did a pretty wonderful job convincing us we wanted to make our home in Pueblo. She's the sort of person when she gets something in her mind it's pretty hard not to end up agreeing with her!

She turned out to be the best boss I ever had in my life, and I'm not an easy person to supervise. What I mean by that is (laughing), arrogantly speaking, I'm a really good psychiatrist and most people who try to supervise me know less than I do, and so I don't respond well to people telling me what to do.

Haydee was different. As a boss, she always made the most of a person's strengths. She was never competitive. She didn't need to be superior because she was the boss. She was always receptive to ideas and clearly wanted to keep good physicians happy and functioning well.

Absolutely she was the best superintendent the hospital ever had. She was the only superintendent ever able to actually speak for the institution and for Pueblo, compared to others who were always under the thumb of the mental health administrators who ran things from Denver. She was just a spunky little lady—she wasn't scared of anything or intimidated by anybody. And she's honest too.

Greg was my direct supervisor initially, and he was so supportive—he was easy to talk to right from the beginning when I was straight out of residency and hadn't been at the state hospital for long. He was a very good mentor and always willing to help out in terms of answering my questions and explaining things. There was never any pressure from him.

Both Greg and Haydee are just wonderful people and very good friends to this day. We go to the symphony and art center together, though for a time they would not come to our house because Haydee does not like dogs and we had dogs, including a huge chocolate Lab that wanted to jump up on our guests. Haydee is a tiny lady and she did not like that at all. She would not come to our house unless we had put the dogs away!

You ask what I think the secret is to Greg and Haydee's successful relationship, personally and professionally. I think the trick is that Greg is not bothered by his wife being a strong professional, "the big boss." He was always more interested in actually practicing psychiatry while she wanted to be an administrative psychiatrist. And of course, they obviously love each other a great deal.

Greg wants to make her happy. I can't really explain how they manage it so well but I think it's because Greg doesn't need to be that "male dominant figure." He thinks so highly of her, and besides, he would not want her job. He recognized that her strength was working for the good of the hospital while his strengths were clinical, working directly for the good of the patients.

Mostly I remember the years and years of having dinners together and enjoying each other's company. I remember Haydee sitting with a group of psychiatrists at the hospital and asking us what she could do that would make the medical staff feel more bonded to the hospital. That led to the staff initiating monthly medical staff dinners. She was always looking for solutions like that to make things better, which is not the way other superintendents acted.

Haydee was able to build camaraderie among the staff, and we became like a big family. Oh, I'm sure there were people to reprimand and things to correct and Haydee did that as needed, but her style was to bring out the best in people and get them to function at the very best level they could.

~

DR. JAY RICHTER: It was a two-fer as far as the Korts were concerned, because they got Elissa and me in one fell swoop! Elissa received financial support as a resident psychiatrist in Denver through a national health service program, which paid for part of her education in exchange for a commitment to work in an underserved area for a period of time. Pueblo was a very under-served area for psychiatry, and Elissa was obligated to stay for two years to pay back her commitment. That's why she took the job, and I tagged along.

It was actually a brilliant strategy on Haydee's part. What she had done was build an alliance with the Department of Psychiatry at the University of Colorado School of Medicine, and as part of that, Elissa and other psychiatry residents would come to Pueblo to complete part of their residency. This was dubbed the "Career Residents Program." It brought energetic, inquisitive, young psychiatrists into Pueblo to live, and to work with patients with unusual and challenging mental health issues. I think it's safe to say that it was pretty universal among the residents who came down to Pueblo that it was a fantastic experience.

And of course, we ended up staying. I took a job at the hospital as a staff physician in the Medicine Department. It was a little bit of a difficult decision coming to Pueblo because I grew up in Boulder and did my medical training in Denver, and we lived in the city for six or seven years and enjoyed all the amenities of living in a metropolitan area.

When we moved to southern Colorado we found a place in a little town called Beulah, up in the mountains. I remember one day driving into Beulah to move some of our belongings from Denver, and on the way I was trying to find an NPR station on the radio and could not, and I thought, "What have we gotten ourselves into?"

After about two years in Pueblo, Haydee promoted me to Chief of Medicine at the hospital. Pueblo was looking more and more like our permanent home.

I remember my first memories of Greg. I was working in the medical-surgical wing of the hospital, and Greg had arranged for the two of us to have regular meetings to discuss ongoing medical matters. I'd walk over to Greg's office in one of the administration buildings and sit down and we would talk. Greg had this way about him that it almost felt like a therapy session. He'd ask, "What's on your mind?" and I'd rattle off my displeasure with the current chief of medicine, or whatever the issue of the day happened to be!

I think our personal friendship with Haydee and Greg happened pretty quickly. Once a month the career residents and the medical staff would get together as a social thing, and we'd rotate as dinner hosts from one person to the next at somebody's house. It was a relaxed setting that cemented relationships between people. That's where we got to know Haydee and Greg pretty well.

I think one of the main things to know about Greg and Haydee Kort is how incredibly supportive they were of the medical staff at the hospital. Their main objective was always to provide the best possible patient care, and they knew that to do that they had to support the physicians and staff who were providing that care. That came through very clearly over the years.

And of course, as superintendent Haydee was a real fighter. She was well known for charging into Denver and really fighting hard for resources for the hospital.

～

Jacquie Huffaker

Jacquie Huffaker worked in the Newspapers in Education program at the Pueblo Chieftain newspaper for twenty-five years. After retiring

*in 2009 she has turned her attention to traveling and regular volun-
teer work at the Pueblo Art Center and at Wednesday Weeders, a
program to beautify public garden spaces around the city. Her husband, Dr. Robert Huffaker, was a psychiatrist at the Colorado State
Hospital. He passed away in 2004.*

I met Haydee and Greg in 1983 shortly after I married my husband, Bob, who was working as a psychiatrist in what was then
called the Colorado State Hospital.

Bob always said that he enjoyed his work at the State Hospital
so much, in great part because Haydee set such high standards for
patient care, and because of her strong support of the staff. She really knew how to advocate for the hospital with the state legislature
too. I have to say, the hospital really flourished under Haydee!

At the time Greg was director of Adult Psychiatric Services, so
Bob worked with him as well. As a couple, Greg and Haydee com-
plemented each other's skills and always supported each other. Of
course, Greg is known for his great sense of humor as well as his
skills as a psychiatrist. Together they are a wonderful couple, and
Bob was very happy to work there.

I was fortunate that Bob was happy there, because that's how
I got to meet Greg and Haydee. The way we became friends was
really because Haydee had started a program that brought career
residents in psychiatry to the State Hospital for a year's residency
program. Bob loved working with the young residents professionally, and he thought it would be a good idea to get to know them
better on a social level too. So the staff started holding monthly
dinners in our homes.

Haydee really supported those dinners, and when they were

held in her house, she must have worked for days preparing a meal—so many wonderful dishes.

Anyway, that's how our friendship began. It was so interesting because at the beginning of the program almost all the residents were male, but within the first two or three years there were more and more female residents. I have to say that to have more women at those dinner parties created a much more vibrant, relaxed and fun atmosphere!

Haydee was a very warm and friendly person. I remember when Bob and I married, she immediately said to Bob, "I want to meet Jacquie" and she invited me to her office, and she was so welcoming. The other strong characteristic I always associate with Haydee is her persistence, particularly when she was considering what was best for the hospital. She had this ability to bring people on board because of her great leadership qualities.

On May 5, 1987, a tragedy changed the lives of Bob and Jacquie Huffaker and horrified people throughout the state. A man suffering from severe paranoia walked into a Pueblo outpatient clinic where Bob was offering psychiatric services and shot Bob between fifteen and eighteen times at close range.

Bob was doing some moonlighting at an outpatient mental health clinic when a patient walked in—of course back then there were no gun control checks at the door—and he opened fire on Bob, saying, "This is for all the years that psychiatry has failed me." Ironically, the patient refused to take medication for his paranoia. Bob told us later he thought he better try to play dead, which he did, and the assailant killed himself. Bob had very extensive injuries, and many surgeries and handicaps for the rest of his life.

Haydee and Greg—I cannot tell you how many ways they responded to help! Haydee called me almost every day to see how he was doing, and she and Greg visited him in the hospital regularly. Haydee kept his job open for him until he could come back to work. That was way over and above what you might expect someone in her position to do.

Bob survived his injuries for seventeen years, and yes, he did go back to work! He had an amazing attitude. He said, "This happens very rarely in the world of psychiatry and I'm going back to work."

Throughout all those years they were very supportive, and invited us a couple of times to join them and other friends at their condo in Vail to have some fun.

But no (laughing), we did not go skiing in Vail! Greg's sports have been racquetball and tennis and Haydee is a talented pianist...so when we went to Vail we just enjoyed being together with friends, and eating and talking and being in that beautiful place. In Pueblo, I've been invited over for tea in the afternoon where Greg and I talk about books and share our recommendations, and Haydee is on the symphony board, and so I see them at the symphony and at the art center.

Of course, what has remained most important to them all these years is family, both here and in Argentina. They have always kept that connection strong.

So yes, I still see Greg and Haydee and enjoy them very much. They have had an impact on many people's lives, and certainly on the life of my husband Bob, and on my own.

∽

John L. Mendoza and Dorothy Mendoza

John L. Mendoza and Dorothy Mendoza are professional artists living in Pueblo, Colorado. John is a landscape artist specializing in romantic paintings of the Southwest and Dorothy is an eclectic artist who enjoys experimenting with different styles. Together throughout the years, they have maintained galleries and studios in Pueblo and Colorado Springs. They currently show their work at the John Deaux Gallery in Pueblo.

∽

DOROTHY: It was the late 1960s when we met, so we've known the Korts over forty years, a long, long time. We have daughters about the same age as Greg and Haydee's children, and we had mutual physician friends, so that's how we came to know them socially.

JOHN: Haydee and Greg collect art privately, and they were interested in what we were doing, so they came by the studio. They liked our work and made it part of their collection and we became very good friends. At that time, my career as a professional artist was very young, and Greg and Haydee were very supportive and encouraging. They didn't just say they liked the paintings (laughing), they actually *bought* them!

DOROTHY: I started painting somewhat later…we've both been professional artists since the 1970s. They have been great at supporting us from the beginning.

We became close enough that for many years we spent every

New Year's Eve together. Every year we watched *Fiddler on the Roof* and played poker. That was our custom on New Year's Eve for years and years and years! We also traveled together, to Santa Fe for the opera, to Reno for the shows and to gamble a bit—we weren't very big gamblers but we were young then and enjoyed that very much.

JOHN: I would have an art show in Santa Fe every year and they would go with us to that too. They're very much Broncos fans too, especially Greg and Marcelo. One year when the Broncos went to the Super Bowl, they had arranged a trip to Argentina and they could not get the score—this was before the Internet—and they were so frustrated that the only scores they could get were soccer scores! It took them days to find out.

DOROTHY: We have so many fond memories. We would go out to eat often. Haydee was great about getting restaurant reservations. She would make up a story: "I'm Dr. Kort and I have the prince-of-so-and-so or the ambassador of Argentina with me tonight, and we would like reservations"—and we always got in.

At one point Haydee's mother came from Argentina to visit. We were talking food and I love to cook, and so do Haydee and her mother. Haydee had to go to work but I went over and cooked an Argentine dish, *matambre* (a flank steak stuffed with vegetables and seasonings), with Haydee's mother. It was a very nice day. Her mother was a wonderful woman. When I had our second baby she crocheted a beautiful dress for her and sent it from Argentina. We had a very loving friendship.

Both Haydee and Greg have been personally very comforting in my life when I was going through a hard time. They helped me when I needed help and were very kind. They always have been supportive, not just in art, but in my personal life, and I owe them for their kindness. It was a matter of talking things out and having that closeness of a good friend.

In recent years, we haven't seen or called each other as frequently but when we do, it's like yesterday. It's that kind of friendship. They are always there for us, and we are there for them.

JOHN: Our friendship has always been like a family.

∽

Thanks to Nell Mitchell, the Historian and Director of the Museum at CMHIP (Colorado Mental Health Institute in Pueblo), and long-term friend of Haydee and Gregorio Kort, who contributed her memories in Chapter 14 and gave generous access to the hospital museum and the Kort Room during the preparation of this book.

Gregorio and Haydee are married July 21, 1957, and in a few days are leaving for the United States.

Haydee's parents, Jose and Sofia Kantorovich

A precious quartet of memories:

Top Left: Newlyweds Haydee and Gregorio ("Goyo and Beba") chat with Haydee's grandmother, Rosa Wernicke at their wedding reception

Top Right: Gregorio's family: Sitting foreground: His parents Abram and Rosa. Standing (l to r): Siblings - Moises, Natalia, Marcos, and Gregorio

Bottom Left: Parents of the bride and groom get together: (l to r) Standing: Abram Kort and Jose Kantorovich; (l to r) Sitting: Rosa Kort and Sofia Kantorovich

Bottom Right: Gregorio's grandparents, Dina and Naftole Turkenich before they left Poland: "My favorite picture of the family."

Gregorio and Haydee's four grandchildren: (Top, l to r): Stephanie and Andrew Kort
BottomL (l to r): Natalia and Sofia Iturri

Haydee's brother, Alberto

The journey from Poland begins: Passport photos of Gregorio's brother Marcos, 10 months old, and his mother, Rosa Kort.

Passport photo of Gregorio's father, Abram, taken in Poland before they left for America

Gregorio and Haydee's son is married: Wedding photo of Marcelo and Allison Kort

A daughter's wedding day: Gabriela (Gabi) Kort weds Joe (Jose) Iturri

Made in the USA
San Bernardino, CA
22 December 2018